LEADERS
with COURAGE

TO: DAVE

You are on excellent leader.

art

ARTHUR E. PUOTINEN

Leaders with Courage by Arthur E. Puotinen

ISBN: 978-1-949712-45-2 (Paperback)
ISBN: 978-1-949712-44-5 (Digital)

Library of Congress Control Number: 2019930797

Printed in the United States of America.

Coffee Press Inc.
138-44C Queens Blvd
Briarwood, New York 11435
https://www.coffeepressny.com

CONTENTS

INTRODUCTION

The State of Illinois had been unable to pass a State Budget for two years in FY 2015 and 2016. Governor Bruce Rauner and State Legislature were unable to agree on an acceptable budget for Illinois. This impasse resulted in a $6.2 billion annual deficit and the state owing businesses, vendors, and social service agencies, $14.7 billion. The two-year delay of promised and needed state funds for various organizations to provide services in the sectors of education, human and social services created major challenges for individual organizations to meet their financial obligations, serve their clientele, and sustain their programs. The threat of receiving a Moody's Investors Services "junk bond" credit rating, growing urgency by educators and other citizens to "Pass the Budget", and movement toward a political resolution, resulted in a special budgetary session for the Illinois legislature in June, 2017.

State Representative Steve Anderson recalled that "on July 2nd, a balanced budget was presented in the House of Representatives, and I voted in favor of it…we faced two options: to vote in favor of the budget, which included an income tax increase, or not vote for the budget and allow the state to fail. Neither were good choices, but stopping the state from falling off a fiscal cliff was the only realistic choice."The budgetary measure proposed a new state budget of $36.5 billion and shifted the personal income tax rate to 4.95 percent from 3.75 percent. Governor Rauner vetoed the measure, but his action was overridden by the necessary votes in the state legislature and "Pass the Illinois Budget" became a reality.

Then in August 2017, the Illinois Legislature passed bipartisan education funding legislation and signed by Governor Bruce Rauner that became a historic breakthrough. Two general state aid payments to schools that should have been made in August were delayed as lawmakers struggled to reach the agreement, due to a provision in the state budget that required a new "evidence-based" funding formula become law before the money could be sent. The new measure allowed the state comptroller to begin sending districts their state aid, and stave off any potential danger of low-income schools shutting down or having to make mid-year cuts.

In the long-term, that new formula stands to level out Illinois' notoriously inequitable way of funding education, by sending more state funds to districts without the local property wealth to fund to "adequately" support students' learning.

A "Fix the Formula" coalition of education advocacy groups sent a statement applauding the compromise: "For the past four years, superintendents, teachers and civil rights leaders have come together to fight for a formula that ensures a student's zip code no longer determines the school resources available."

The package guarantees every district will receive at least as much in the future as it did this year; going forward, any additional money will be put through the new evidence-based formula.

Additionally, Illinois will begin to pick up the tab for Chicago Public Schools' teachers' retirement benefits, as it does for every other district. Chicago also gains the ability to raise the local property tax rate, which is estimated to bring in up to $120 million that can be used for CPS pensions.

House Speaker Michael Madigan said in a statement: "Through compromise, we've included some provisions that many members would not have supported on their own. But a package that permanently provides more money for Illinois schools and puts us closer than ever to fixing Illinois' broken school funding system is too important to let partisan differences get in the way."

When organizational leaders face financial crises, how should they and/or how do they respond to them? Their responses express their leadership style and courage in making decisions that shape their organizational future and ongoing practices. Many stories can be told about why and how the Illinois Budget crisis began, continued, and was resolved.

Leadership Challenges

The purpose of this book is to document leadership experiences and practices of certain organizations dealing with delays in the Illinois Budget passage. This record relates to promised/designated State funding to education, social services, and faith-based organizations with a focus on the Kane County, Illinois region.

For this book, I have chosen to focus on the personal stories of six organizational leaders who experienced the delay in Illinois state funding for their institutions. They lived through the stress of disappointment and uncertainty to bring personal courage, initiative, and constructive action to their groups, region, and state. The principals or players in this book are the following top-level leaders, with date of my interviews with each of them:

Mark Stutrud, Executive Director, Lutheran Social Services of Illinois	11.9.2017
Kelly Aurand, Director, Bethlehem Child Development Center, Elgin IL	1.23.2018
Tony Sanders, CEO, U-46 District Schools, Elgin, IL	12.20.2017
Dr. David Sam, President, Elgin Community College, Elgin IL	2.7.2018

| Jaime Garcia, Executive Director, Centro de Informacion, Elgin, IL | 1.18.2018 |
| Michele Meyer, Director, Mutual Ground, Aurora, IL | 2.16.2018 |

These six leaders agreed to be interviewed for this book and to share their stories. I know each of them and became familiar with their work and leadership. As former pastor of Bethlehem Lutheran Church in Elgin during 2005-2013, I worked closely with Kelly Aurand and associated with Tony Sanders, Dr. David Sam, and Jaime Garcia as fellow members of the Elgin Noon Rotary Club. My knowledge of Mark Stutrud's work grows from my being a member of the LSSI Cornerstone Foundation Committee since 2016. While serving as Interim Pastor of Our Savior Lutheran Church in Aurora, IL during 2016 to 2017, I visited the Mutual Ground facilities and learned about Michele Meyer's important work. Together, these six leaders have a diversity of backgrounds, talents, and organizations. I thank them for their participation in this writing project and commend them for their excellent leadership and dedicated service to their communities.

Format of This Book

This book began early in the morning of October 23, 2017. I awakened with ideas and inspiration. My first book "Lead With Courage: Unleash the Lion in You" (Balboa Press, 2015), was a memoir, self-help book, and I felt that it needed to be followed with stories of other leaders. I came up with the book title, "Leaders with Courage", and added "Pass the Budget" for focus and urgency to the selected information.

The research method involved developing an interview format with questions. This approach worked well in the Suomi College (now Finlandia University) Oral History project that involved interviews of older residents living in the mining regions of Upper Michigan and

Minnesota (see pages 204 to 205, in "Lead with Courage" for interview format).

With a burst of enthusiasm that October morning, I developed the following questions for the six persons to be interviewed:

Template of Topics for Interviews

Personal Background and Perspectives

1. Brief Biographical Statement
2. Preparation and Process for Leadership Position
3. Perspective on Essentials for Excellent Leadership

Crisis Dimensions resulting from Illinois State Budget Delay

1. What are the state-funded items in your budget? Note specific types of subsidies.
2. What is the amount of delayed payment or shortfall of state funding you have experienced?
3. Give an example(s) of this delay or loss in the lives of those you serve and lead.

Coping Strategies (A – G)

Advocate

1. How has your organization presented its funding needs to the governor and legislature?
2. What individual approaches have you taken with the governor and legislature?
3. What steps have you taken to inform your clients and constituents about the budget delay?

Balance the Budget

1. What process do you follow to build a budget for the coming year?
2. Do you build in a reserve fund or contingency fund to cope with state budget funding delays?
3. Has the state fund delay created a crisis mindset in your organization?

Care for Clients

1. Have you needed to cut some programs and reduce your staff? Give example(s)
2. How have you focused your organizational strategies to fulfill your mission?
3. How does your leadership team work together and assist other staff members in their work and plans?

Decide New Strategies

1. How have you changed your strategic plan during State funding delays?
2. What valuable information and assistance did you receive from workshops, consultants, etc.?
3. Describe new initiatives and activities you developed to maintain, change, and/or eliminate services.

Exert Effort to Succeed

1. How did you as a leader motivate and mobilize your team members to respond to the budget shortfall?
2. Give examples of activities that worked and did not work?
3. What personal resources did you have to maintain your own energy and effort?

Find Funds and Friends

1. Describe various fund-raising activities your organization used to meet financial needs?
2. How did you communicate your organizational story to constituents, donors, and prospects?
3. What are the key elements to having a successful outreach during a critical time period?

Give Thanks

1. Is gratitude important during a difficult time for you and your organizations?
2. Describe various ways you and your organization give thanks to friends and supporters.
3. What lessons in leadership have you learned throughout this crisis?

Preparations for Interviews and Research

In November and December 2017, I began preliminary interviews with the six leaders. In my visits with them, I presented them with a gift copy of "Lead With Courage: Unleash the Lion in You", and encouraged them to review "Chapter Nine; Recover from a Crisis" that relates the impact of the Flood of 1993 in Des Moines and its impact on many organizations, including Grand View College. I explained the purpose of the new book would beto tell their stories of leadership during challenging times. They had valuable insights to share with local and larger audiences. I gave them a copy of the interview questions as topics for their interviews and sought their agreement for a future time to be interviewed.

The research method included initial review of some public record documents of each organization before and during oral interviews with key leaders regarding the above topics.

The interviews took place on the following timetable, and I recorded the hour-long interview with them in the respondent's business location as follows:

Subsequent transcription of interviews into written documents by this writer, took place and the respondents received initial drafts of their interview. I continued to edit the six drafts and provided the leaders with their upgraded interviews, inviting them to complete a final review of their chapter. They did so and offered clarifications and additions to make the chapter in their own words. Also included, are information about the organization's mission and services, budgetary revenue and public records.

CHAPTER ONE

U-46 SCHOOL DISTRICT, ELGIN ILLINOIS
CHIEF EXECUTIVE OFFICER
TONY SANDERS

Chief Executive Officer Tony Sanders runs the day-to-day operations of School District U-46, a place he has called home since 2007. Mr. Sanders oversees the implementation of all Board and District policies and procedures as well as alignment of resources to all District initiatives and improvement plans for the state's second-largest school district. He works in close collaboration with an administrative staff that manages a balanced District budget of more than $500 million, and he was a leader in the successful state-wide effort to pass equitable state education funding.

A leader known for his diligence, hands-on and collaborative approach, Mr. Sanders works with staff and community members to implement goals supporting the District's Strategic Plan which calls for ensuring all students gain the experiences they need to graduate from School District U-46 prepared to contribute and compete in a global society. He's proud of the District's many achievements, from high schools ranked among the best in the country, to a thriving dual-language program and expanding early childhood educational opportunities.

Mr. Sanders serves as the Chair of the Large Countywide and Suburban Consortium, a network of some of the nation's most successful district leaders. Under Mr. Sanders's tenure at CEO, U-46 has implemented universal full-day kindergarten, expanded Dual Language and Gifted programming, provided additions to three elementary schools and implemented several new comprehensive curriculum resources. The District began implementing a trauma-informed care approach to responding to behavioral issues and supporting students. Next year, the District will expand its award-winning Dual Language program to the high school level.

Prior to becoming CEO in 2014, Mr. Sanders served as the Chief of Staff for former Superintendent Dr. José M. Torres. Mr. Sanders joined the District as Chief Communications Officer after holding the same title in St. Louis Public Schools. He brings two decades of leadership experience to his current post, having served as Acting Director for Governmental Relations and Public Information for the Illinois State Board of Education and other top posts at the Department of Professional Regulation and the Illinois Department of Public Health.

Mr. Sanders earned his Master of Business Administration degree from New York Institute of Technology–Ellis College, and his undergraduate degree from the University of Illinois at Springfield.

My Early Mentors

I was born in New Mexico in Albuquerque, New Mexico to two parents who were teachers. My father was a junior high math teacher and my mom was a music teacher. They met in college, and after getting married, they did their student teaching together at a Navajo Indian reservation. They had four kids, and I'm the youngest of four.

My father ended up leaving the classroom, though, and working as a state leader in education. He was a deputy superintendent in New Mexico and then state superintendent of schools in Nevada. When I was in high school, we moved to Illinois for him to be the state superintendent of education in Illinois. My parents were obviously very strong influences on my life. They both had the passion about teaching and mentoring youth, and it showed up throughout their careers.

I had resisted that path of being a teacher, but my older sister became a teacher. I never saw my role as being that of an educator. I wanted to be a DJ. If you remember the TV show WKRP in Cincinnati, I wanted to be on the radio as the next Dr. Johnny Fever. My parents, God bless them, never discouraged me from pursuing my dream. In college, I studied communications and dreamed of being on the radio. My first career was actually on the radio in Springfield, Illinois on the state's top country music station WFMB. One thing my parents didn't instill in me though was the desire to seek and find out what particular jobs pay before you get your degree in that field. I discovered quickly that disc jockeys don't make a lot of money.

The lessons in leadership particularly in education, I learned as a small child, specifically from my father as a classroom teacher. When I was eight years old and onward, he was the state superintendent of schools and I learned really the politics of public education, especially at the state board level. A key lesson from my father was the importance of public education as the cornerstone of our democratic society. Second, I also realized your relationships matter to be able to get along with other people, whether it's your bosses or those who work directly for you. Third, people are always watching your every move to see how you react.

These three lessons from my father impacted my ability to lead U-46 during the state budget crisis in Illinois. The power of relationships in knowing people in Springfield at the capital and locally to figure out politically the best people to approach about the problems that we faced helped prepare me for the challenges ahead.

Getting Started at U-46

I came to U-46 in 2007. The superintendent of the time Connie Neale hired me in July, and in my very first meeting with her in this office she said, "I'm sick, and I have to take a leave of absence." So, I had literally just been hired and had no boss. I worked with the U-46 board very closely as they decided on the process to follow in selecting the next superintendent. They gave me an active role, not a deciding role obviously, but the board very quickly had faith in me to help lead the firm that was doing the search work.

The board hired José Torres who ended up being another phenomenal mentor. I've never worked for anybody longer in my career than I did for José Torres. For seven years we worked and faced a difficult financial situation. When he became superintendent here in 2008, everybody in this district was under the impression that we had firm financial footing and everything was going very well. The prior year it was announced that U-46 was "back in the black" on solid financial footing, and everybody was having a celebration.

Then two things happened at that time. (1) The board decided to move away from the cash basis of accounting to modified accrual. In doing so, they uncovered that we were pushing some bills off into the next fiscal year on a regular basis. So, if you actually looked and saw how much your budget would bring in and expend within the same school year, that meant we were about $19 million short. (2) Then the housing market collapses and the Consumer Price Index at the rate of inflation came in at the lowest point ever of 0.01. It sent school districts across the United States in a tailspin because of the reliance on local property taxes, the amount of the consumer price index determines how much you can get in property tax increases.

Budget Crisis in 2009

U-46 was quickly facing a $40 million budget shortfall in 2009. We did a reduction in force of 1100 teachers, and 700 permanently lost their jobs. Class sizes skyrocketed. We drained our swimming pools for half of the year. We reduced art, music and PE programs. We reduced administrators. We outsourced some operations. It was really a bad fiscal time and ended by setting the stage for the work that came here in the state of Illinois and its own fiscal crisis. It came at the worst time, right after school districts and social service agencies had already gone through massive cuts. Then to have the state continuing to struggle made it more difficult for anybody in the public sector.

Regarding funding sources for U-46 there are three principal sources of revenue: local property taxes, State of Illinois subsidies, and federal funds. Looking at the last four years the federal funds have been fairly flat to steady and don't increase a lot. Property taxes have gone up because when the state can't pay its bills the only thing that will go up is your property taxes. The last two fiscal years, we've been able to not increase taxes in the aggregate except for new construction and we're giving taxpayers a little bit of a break from seeing the tax increase. One of the anomalies that frustrates taxpayers is when the housing market collapses and their housing value of their property decreased, the taxes on their property went up. But that's the way our property tax system is. If the value of their property drops there is an inverse relationship between the property values and the tax rates. Your property values go down, and the tax rate goes up because property taxes don't go away, they keep growing and it's hard for people. This is the only time that I know of in our nation's history where housing values were going down at the same time property taxes are going up. That's why you see especially in Illinois this rallying cry to freeze property taxes because that's not what's supposed to happen.

Student Enrollment Trends and State Funding

Demographic trends have an impact on state funding of schools. Student enrollment has changed in U-46. When I first got here in 2007, we were still more than 50 percent white and that has quickly become more than 50 percent Latino and about 30 percent white. Our other populations have stayed the same. Leading up to 2007, this district grew by leaps and bounds. They were there adding a thousand plus kids every school year. When I first got here, we just opened South Elgin High School and Canyon Woods Middle School, and two more elementary schools just opened up.

Then with the housing market crash we've seen students migrate out. They graduate, but they're not being replaced by newer kids which means that our neighborhoods have not "churned". The term means that, usually, people will raise their family and downsize to another community. Those families are not moving, however, so we're not seeing a lot of new kids coming into the neighborhoods. Enrollments are starting to trickle down about 400 to 500 kids per year.

Illinois Budget Crisis

Right after the market crashed, the federal money put in place to subsidize state school districts through the American Recovery and Reinvestment Act in 2009–2011 started to fade away just as Governor Rauner was elected. He had an agreement with the legislature that they would go in and reduce the state's budget at the end of the fiscal year. That was the first tell there were significant issues to take place. Once the state has appropriated general state aid money for public education, they must make those payments. The only option to not make those payments is to change that appropriation at the legislative level and reduce it. That's exactly what happened right after Governor Rauner was elected and found out what a mess the state finances were in. We were in the tail end of my first year as the leader of the organization when we find out that the state is going to cut 5 percent of our general state aid at the end of the school year.

There's nothing we can do about it, no cuts that we can make. In the school year, we have paid out our teacher salaries, and we have made staffing decisions for the next school year. We have no recourse, there's nothing left to cut. Luckily, we had enough reserve funds to cover that year, but this situation was the first sign that we had to really start paying attention to what was happening at the state level. It's always been an issue but not to that degree.

Three Types of State Aid

There were different segments of state aid that were coming in to local school districts. Twelve different funds were detailed in this process, and the biggest one is the general state aid, which is the only piece of school funding that was means tested, meaning that school districts would get a percentage based on their ability to raise funds locally. The second piece was this what they call the supplemental general state aid which is just a simple calculation of how many low-income kids you have in your district. It results in a dollar amount for each of those kids. Then the third pot of state aid is called mandated categoricals. Those refer to specific programs like special education, bilingual education, early childhood education, and transportation. These three big buckets are on a reimbursement basis. When the state can't afford to pay its bills, it's the mandated categoricals that they stop paying. There is no law that says they have to pay them and so that's one of those that we have to try to figure out whether or not we put them in the budget every year or if we don't put them in.

If you put them in a budget for a district of our size, it amounts to about $8 million every quarter that we should be paid. They kind of went away; sometimes we get them and sometimes we wouldn't.

Budgetary Adjustments and Cuts

When funding is not available, it causes considerable stress in an organization and leads to difficult decisions and adjustments to be made. In 2009, when we had made all those massive reductions, cutting art, music, PE, and everything else, we increased our class sizes to twenty-eight kids per teacher in grades kindergarten through second and thirty-three kids per teacher in grades three through six. That is a lot of kids in the classroom. That was the standard for ideal class-size we used to staff our schools. I don't think any parent would ever say that thirty-three kids in a classroom is a good idea. But this is what we had to do coming on the heels of the major meltdown. What do we cut next when there's nothing left to cut? So, we delayed bus purchases. We restructured our internal debt to get a working cash bond just to continue to make ends meet. Like a family facing a similar crisis where somebody suddenly has her salary decreased and your expenditures are fixed, you can't stop making your house payment or they will come after you. You have to pay your water and electric bills. You were not a position to get a second job as a school district so our only option was to borrow against our equity. We borrowed against future tax payments to keep afloat. We took out a loan. Many families had to do it during that same period of time.

New Educational Programs

Some good things can happen even though times are difficult. Despite major budget cuts even back to 2009, we invested in new programs like Advancement Via Individual Determination, which is really a program designed for students who are typically B or C average students.

We know they can do better and this program takes these students and invests in their ability to learn to a great degree with the goal of getting them into Advanced Placement by the time they get to high school. We invested in our dual language program and took advantage of our demographics to change our school system. We took the power of that second language that so many of our students were bringing in to turn it into an award-winning dual language program. Starting next year, it rolls into the high school, and we will be one of the few districts across the country that is graduating students both bilingual and biliterate when they walk out of our doors. We continue to invest in gifted education making sure that we still were serving kids that needed those higher-level courses.

For my first couple of years in my role is that I ended up spending so much more time focused on state government, the state legislature and getting a funding formula change that I missed out on what was happening in our classrooms. My regret is I did not visit every school as frequently as I wanted to visit and think that's how you really influence instruction right is by visiting classrooms and seeing what was actually going on in classrooms. This year we have a state funding fix to allow me to spend more of my time in classrooms than ever before.

U-46 Strategic Plan and State Funding

I think the biggest thing for me when I first came into this role was we developed a new strategic plan for the school district. The Board of Education set as a strategic priority to seek a change in the way the state funds public education. Our board demands through the strategic plan that we do something in Springfield to change the state funding. They gave me the political cover to not worry about having a Board of Education complain about any of my activities. I could point back to the strategic plan that they approved and say that you told me to do this work. Without that, it would've been a lot more difficult to take some of the risks that we had to take to try to get a change in the state funding formula.

Superintendents for Equity First

As soon as I took this role, we got involved with a state-wide advocacy group called Superintendents for Equity First. As a member of that group, I started spending more time in Springfield advocating and testifying before committees about the need for more state funding. The biggest thing that led our school district to change our funding process by the state because it couldn't afford to pay the entirety of that general state aid. They would do an across-the-board per-pupil cut from general state aid which they call proration, and that proration then hit different districts differently and inequitably. For example, every time they couldn't pay the full amount of general state aid District U-46 would lose $400 for every kid we serve. But if you look at St. Charles just down the road but wealthier, they would lose $60 per kid. In Barrington, they would lose $40 because they don't rely on general state aid. So, it was that state proration that really led to legislators to realize how inequitable our school funding formula is. This fact became the pain point and the wake-up call for at least the state level that they had to make a change.

I worked with fellow superintendents to do our best for the first three years. The first few bills we worked on with the state legislature all had one common problem. The earliest proposals took money away from wealthy districts and redistributed it to poor districts. In Springfield, though, that Robin Hood approach doesn't sell well. When you're a politician trying to be reelected, no politician wants to come back home and say our school district is going to lose money so that U-46 can gain money. That's where the conversation stopped.

The key to the solution was finally going to require all districts to at least understand they don't lose any money in the first year. That is the bill that passed in which no district loses money this very first year. The challenge for the state is to come up with an additional $300 million per year every year. Whether or not the state can actually afford that price tag for having a fixed formula will be interesting to see.

Advocacy by Mobilization of Superintendents

On the issue of passing the Illinois State budget in general, I worked with the superintendents and had a meeting with the governor and worked with his Secretary of Education. Ultimately, what happened is we were trying to fix the school funding formula, but without a state budget behind it, the effort is meaningless. So, with our partners in higher education and social service agencies not having a budget for several years in a row, I met with a group of superintendents in 2017 including Karen Sullivan (Indian Prairie), Jeff Craig (Aurora West), and Jennifer Garrison from downstate Illinois. We decided to do a statewide push and do a grassroots movement of superintendents. I gained access to every superintendents' email address across the state, and we sent them a message saying would you join us in this fight? We're going to ask for three things: (1) to pass a state budget not just for K-12 education, but a full state budget; (2) to improve the school funding formula; and (3) to pay districts what you owe them. We did it under the social media hashtag of #PassILBudget. We launched, and before long we had districts joining us. We were able to get Chicago and Rockford public schools in really early. When superintendents started hearing about our movement, I was getting emails and it blew up my email and actually shut down my emails in U-46. I still have a picture on my phone that I had exceeded my email limit within our school district. When they shut my email down, I called the information services director and said, "Do you really want your CEO not having email access?"

Meeting with Legislative Leaders

We trended on social media across the nation and were the second trending story of the day, right behind President Obama's return to Chicago. He gave a speech that same day at the University of Chicago. As result of this coalition building, we were able to get a meeting scheduled with the four legislative leaders and the governor. We had asked for the meetings to be held together, but what we did get was individual meetings with the four legislative leaders and the governor. They all agreed to meet with us on the same day so that we didn't have to make multiple trips.

We met with Speaker Madigan, Senate President Cullerton, Governor Rauner and with the two Republican leaders to share our message. They all pointed back at the other person with accusations we see in the newspaper. Madigan blamed the governor who blamed Madigan for the budgetary impasse, and we said it's basically all of your fault.

The tipping point was reached when we hit about 200 superintendents signing on to the campaign. Our goal was 200 superintendents out of 800 plus, so when we reached 200, we realized that we have something here and the list continued to grow and reached more than 400. Two-thirds of the students across the state of Illinois around 1.4 million represented the districts of school superintendents who signed on to the campaign. We estimate that the reason why this trended on social media is that we gave everybody a bullet list of things they had to do. The biggest one was to change the marquee on your school sign to say "Pass Illinois Budget." Put it on your home page of your website and change your profile picture. Overnight, the picture started popping up of people changing the signs over to say Pass Illinois Budget. Churches did it, schools did it and it just became like a movement. I think that's why the legislative leaders agreed to meet with us because you could not be in any part of the state without some sign saying Pass Illinois Budget.

The Tipping Point of Pass the Illinois Budget

Remember the movie *Oh God* with George Burns, and the second one was called *Oh God Book II*. It had this little girl that started a campaign called Think God and everybody started putting "Think God" on their signs. It reminded me of how our campaign just kept spreading. Before long people jumped on this movement. Relationships matter. Within the boundaries of U-46 we have eleven legislative districts between the Illinois Senate and House so there's eleven legislators represent us on every day in Springfield when they are there. I should have given them a heads up that this is what we were doing. There was some level of knowledge among some of our legislators that we were building this campaign together, but I should've had the foresight to realize the impact that it would have on our local legislators. Whenever this hits everywhere and, in their neighborhoods, where they have to be voted into office, these signs were popping up everywhere. With 20/20 hindsight, I would've taken the step to make sure everybody knew this is what we're doing and this is why we're doing it at the state level before we launched.

Taking a Stand for Equity

What turned the corner was this recognition that we're not going to take this delay anymore and that the state has to have a budget. I started making public and sending to our coalition superintendents some little facts about the lack of a state budget and what it is meant actually for state government. During this time that the state doesn't have a budget to pay social service agencies and to fund higher education, they are still buying millions of dollars in vehicles without a state appropriation. The state of Illinois had different agencies with appropriations to run these agencies. No prisons or state agencies closed because of a lack of a state budget. They were still buying cars and still hiring people. I asked the question, which is more important, a teacher or a prison guard? The state never shut down although they shut down everybody else or dramatically impacted them, but the state itself suffered no ill effect from the lack of a state budget. To this day, this is one of the most infuriating things.

Passing the State Budget Makes a Difference

By passing a state budget in August we actually ended up getting enough revenue in to make our FY 2017 budget balanced, even though it was not projected to be that way. Then the new state budget is coupled with the evidence-based funding formula that the state legislature passed. It ended up being $22 million plus another $1.8 million for bilingual education. We are going to be in a much better position moving forward, and the conversations now with the board will be how we best invest dollars to serve kids. We don't have enough money after this year set aside for capital improvements, so we need to set some aside for capital projects. Remember all those cuts we made back in 2009. Here we are coming up on 2018 almost a decade later to ask what we reinvest in to best serve kids. That's a great conversation I can't wait to have.

Organizational Strategies

When lacking a state budget, we didn't have the money to add additional administrators, and it was a challenge even thinking about adding another position to the organizational structure. My team has been overly worked. When you're with 40,000 kids and 56 school buildings, people can look at the organizational structure and think that we're over staffed. We're not overstaffed. I have one assistant superintendent for twenty-one elementary schools and another assistant superintendent for twenty-one elementary schools. How can anybody in the end look at that number and say, oh yeah, one person can oversee twenty-one principals plus the students in those schools and actually be effective. That's a hard sell.

I created two deputy positions: a deputy for instruction that oversees all the school activities to try to alleviate some of the burden on the other systems and then a deputy over operations to help me with the transportation, food service, and other details. It lightens my load a little bit in terms of appraisals and alignment of the full system. It's a big district and I like for us to feel small. But it's not lost on me that with 2500 teachers, over 4000 staff members and 56 different schools in 90 square miles. There are a lot of moving parts.

When I looked at some of the organization's other school districts of similar size to see how they organize, and I just realized that I needed a deputy superintendent. I am not being an educator by training. I never went to school to learn how to do curriculum and it is not my expertise. So, on the instruction side, I need somebody as a deputy that can really focus on instruction.

Caring for Clients

Despite the state budget situation, we still decided to invest in a full-day kindergarten. I believe that will be a game changer for so many of our kids. Last year, we had 2800 full-day kindergarten students. Because we added full-day kindergarten, I also made sure that every elementary school had a full-time social worker. They all had a social worker part-time, and now they all have a social worker full-time. This not a perfect situation because we still have some social and emotional needs that we're not meeting. Our poverty rate has increased so dramatically over the last decade. We have kids coming to us with so much trauma in their lives that school is the one safe place that they have. It is the one place where we can make a difference. Adding those two elements, full-day kindergarten and social work support, in the long term will have great payoff for communities. I hope we can have more in the future.

Motivating Our Team Members to Succeed

We went through a year where the teachers took a pay freeze and administers took two years of pay freezes. We've never made those up. I know that some people don't like the thought of giving raises to public servants. It is assumed that we should do this work just because we're good people. But the fact is that we do have to pay people for the work they do. We have to motivate them and sometimes that motivation does come in the form of a paycheck increase. Yes, we're giving raises this year.

One of the things that I have tried to do throughout my career to motivate employees is a weekly message for employees. It is a nice personal touch for people to know in a large district or large organization that the leader actually shares where we're going and what we're doing. People need to know the why behind your decisions. I've encouraged every person I worked with in the past to do a weekly message of outlining "the why". Each one has approached it differently.

Since I came into this role, I deliberately try to not make it about me. It's not about where I've been and which schools I visited. Every now and again you will see me touch the great things I have seen in a school, but it's more about here's where we are. Throughout this budget process or lack of a state budget, you can go back and read my messages. Many of them focus on the lack of a state budget and what that means for us as a school district, just making sure people know what to expect. Part of the weekly message is praise and part is giving them the why we do what we do. The commendation of specific individuals is the kudos section, and people love the kudos at the bottom of the message. I think they bypass my personal reflections sometimes on purpose to go straight to see if their name is listed in the kudos.

Finding Funds and Friends

We have an educational foundation that raises funds and had some success. When Dr. Torres was here, he started the superintendent scholarship. I've continued to raise money for the scholarship. It's not a program but it's an effort to find funds so we can give thousand-dollar scholarships to kids that are the first in their family to go to college and are graduating from U-46. Every year that effort just grows, and I am so pleased and blessed that people will step up to fund a scholarship for a kid. Last January we raised $33,000 for scholarships, the biggest amount we ever received. Let's see if we can beat it this year. This project is just near and dear to me. I find it so amazing to think that I had a hand in graduating students from U-46, but also that thirty of them last year will go off to college and have a portion of it paid. Hundreds of kids have gotten scholarships to go on and that makes you feel good.

Giving Thanks and Gratitude

Giving thanks to friends and supporters is important during a difficult time, and the kudos newsletter has helped. Other things that leaders can do is go out and visit key people. For example, we had a storm hit my first year as CEO right at the tail end of the school day. Our buses had picked up our elementary kids and were trying to get them home when the storm came. It suddenly burst out of nowhere, with wind and lightning that downed power lines and trees. An extraordinary amount of time was needed to get them home. One bus had a branch of a tree fall on it. No kids were on the bus, but the driver had glass that got in her hair, and it was just a bad afternoon for our bus drivers. The storm knocked out power for two days; it happened on Friday. Coming back to work that Monday, I got up extra early and went out to our bus department to shake the hand of every one of our four hundred bus drivers as they came in for work that morning. They care about our kids and made sure every kid got home safe.

It's that personal touch, not just putting it in a newsletter, but the physical act of saying thank you to somebody is important. I try to do it for other groups when things happen. I'll go visit them and say thank you.

Lessons in Leadership

The biggest lesson came within the last year. I live in the school district, my kids have gone to school in this district, and my son graduated last May with the Larkin High School Class of 2017. I realize that this job, if I had to do it over, I would be more conscious of the toll it takes on a person's family. I was so caught up in leading and trying to do the right thing and take care of everybody. When you get on an airplane, you get those lessons about fastening your seatbelt, putting your facemask on first before you put somebody else's on them. I should have been putting the mask on myself and taking care of myself and my family before I try to take care of 56 schools and 40,000 kids, and I miss that. If I could do it over the last four years I would've spent more time trying to make sure to care for my wife Schelli and my children Jack and Lexie. I missed a lot.

Illinois School District U-46

School District U-46 serves nearly 40,000 children in grades pre-K–12. The District ranks as the second largest in Illinois with forty elementary schools, eight middle schools and five high schools.

Elgin School District U-46 serves families in eleven communities across ninety square miles within Chicago's northwest suburbs. The District is nestled in the Fox River Valley, approximately forty-five minutes west of downtown Chicago, and includes communities within Cook, DuPage and Kane counties.

Middle school students attend Abbott, Canton, Eastview, Ellis, Kenyon Woods, Kimball, Larsen or Tefft schools. Thereafter they enroll in Bartlett, Central School programs, Dream Academy, Elgin, Larkin, South Elgin, or Streamwood high schools.

More than 39,000 preschoolers through twelfth graders attend the 57 District schools and programs. The student population lists 103 different languages spoken at home, and more than half of U-46 students are from Hispanic families.

Mission

Our mission is to be a great place for all students to learn, all teachers to teach, and all employees to work. All means *all*.

Strategic Plan

In 2014, a Strategic Plan Steering Committee made up of staff, parents and community members, began working on establishing a new vision for School District U-46. Nearly a year later, in April 2015, the Board of Education approved a new U-46 Strategic Plan featuring four aspirations and eight related priorities.

Each of the following four aspirations identified two priorities for future achievement:

- Student Achievement
- Effective and Engaged Staff
- Community Engagement
- Excellence, Efficiency & Accountability

The Strategic Plan Steering Committee developed measurable goals to meet the aspirations and priorities over the next several years.

U-46 Operating Revenues for
Years Ended on December 31

	2017	**2016**
Local Sources	$321.1 Million	$316.8 Million
State Sources	$149.7 Million	$158.1 Million
Federal Sources	$ 38.2 Million	$ 37.2 Million
Total Revenue	$509.1 Million	$512.1 Million

U-46 Enrollment Data

	2017	2016
Total Student Enrollment	$39,377	$39,903
Teaching Staff	$ 2,504	$ 2,489

CHAPTER TWO

BETHLEHEM LUTHERAN CHILD DEVELOPMENT CENTER ELGIN, ILLINOIS DIRECTOR KELLY AURAND

Getting Started at CDC

I started working here at the Child Development Center the summer after my freshman year of college. I was the school-age teacher and my responsibilities included planning lessons and activities for the summer program. Every year, while I was at Winona State University, I came back as the school-age teacher and really enjoyed it. I looked forward to seeing the teachers and all of the kids that would attend each summer. My major was elementary education with a pre-primary focus so CDC's preschool program interested me as well. After graduating from college, I sent out over fifty resumes and applications to different school districts because essentially, I wanted to become an elementary school teacher. Talk about disheartening, I received one letter back after everything that was sent out, saying sorry, the position you have applied for has been filled. So, I have this degree in elementary education and what can be done?

Lo and behold, the assistant director position opened up at the Child Development Center, and I was willing to give it a try. After graduating from Winona State University in Minnesota I began as the assistant director here at CDC in 2004 and then quickly worked my way up to director in 2006. The previous director had just resigned, and I was almost thrown into the director role. I was ready for it, although I didn't have much experience. I knew the ins and outs of the daycare, the families and also that I needed a lot to learn like the business perspective of the daycare. And I did.

CDC Organization

The CDC is a ministry of Bethlehem Lutheran Church, and my immediate supervisor is its pastor. I report any concerns or good news to the pastor first. I also meet with a Board of Directors that is appointed at the annual BLC congregational meeting. The seven board members all have different experiences and occupations, and they are able to bring valuable resources to the child development center. We have retired teachers and some members in financial fields that help with the budget. We have Toya Randall, a CDC parent, that brings the outreach part of the daycare to the table in partnership and fundraising. She works with different foundations where she's had experiences. I report all my weekly daily activities to the CDC board and with their recommendations and their help, we run the childcare effectively.

I don't do this by myself. Our assistant director Amanda Richoz has been here at CDC for twenty-three years and is the lead teacher in the infant and toddler classroom. We also have nine other staff members in infant care, two-year-old care, a three-year-old classroom, pre-K program, a full-day kindergarten program and afterschool program, as well as a summer program.

Financial Support from the State of Illinois

Another important partner with CDC is the state of Illinois primarily through two relationships. We are licensed through the Department of Children and Family Services, and we are visited annually by a DCFS representative that comes in to make sure that we are following all of the guidelines and procedures outlined in their handbook. For the last twenty-three years, we have been licensed through DCFS, and they help us provide quality care for the children.

The other aspect of how we work with the state is through the Illinois Department of Human Services. Their program is for parents, single moms, and moms trying to go to school to provide them with an opportunity to receive state assistance and be able to pay for their childcare. Childcare is not cheap, and we would like those families to have childcare as well. Currently at CDC 25 percent of our families are subsidized by the state of Illinois. We've done quite a shift over the last year or so. We used to be about 50 percent subsidized and cut that in half in the recent year. CDC receives a monthly reimbursement at the end of every month that pays for childcare to parents that meet state guidelines. To qualify for this assistance a parent must maintain a steady job and submit payroll stubs for approval through the state before receiving funding.

Caring for CDC Children and Families

Presently CDC enrolls sixty-two students enrolled from a diverse community of learners. They represent some church members and also members from surrounding communities. Culturally, we have Caucasian,

Hispanic, African-American, and Asian with some biracial families. The family profile includes two parents, one parent, foster parents as well as children that have been adopted. We serve everyone because we are a mission of the Evangelical Lutheran Church in America. Some people assume that you have to be a practicing Lutheran to enroll, but that's not the case. We are open to anybody. We do teach and practice Christian values. Yet we do not exclude any children if they have another faith practice to follow.

The keys to success in managing and running our CDC are to maintain a friendly yet professional partnership with each of the families. You have to be open and have good communication to layout rules and expectations. You have to be willing to bend a little bit as well and recognize various financial issues or other issues going on at home. You need to keep open lines of communication with parents and make sure that both of you really have what's in the best interest of the child.

My passion for leadership as the CDC Director has grown. I always wanted to be a teacher, but then after doing this for so many years, I realized the necessity for it. That keeps me driven to do so. Families come to me and say, "We visited another daycare and we like you guys much better." When I hear things like that it makes me want to keep on going. Directing this type of program is not an easy field. We face many challenges, and you can have your good days and your bad days. Overall, as a center, we are a very good team and serve the community well.

What happens on a really good day is when everybody shows up to work, nobody is sick, all the children are here in good health and good spirits. The children have fun with lots of different programs that we are offering them right now. In one of those good programs that come here, we see the children having fun and the teachers engaging with them. The parents are excited to pick up their children, and they actually have a conversation with them. They say how is your day today, can you tell me something fun that you did? Then everybody goes home on their merry way and does their family stuff. In general, a good day is everybody learning, having fun, being healthy and happy.

Setback in State Support

A bad day for the Child Development Center was the time the state of Illinois budget was delayed. Several years ago, the state did not pass the budget. There was a shortfall, and we were not getting paid for a certain amount of time the children were here. They were not very forthcoming about letting you know that they have these hardships. It's like a carpet being pulled out from underneath you. You are moving right along; you think you're fully enrolled with all these children coming in. You will just be financially successful for that year. Then the state says sorry, we can't pay you for three months of care for the twenty-five students that you have enrolled at your school. That's a shock. We operate as a nonprofit organization so all of the tuition that comes in goes right to our expenses. We actually ended up having the church support us, for we had to take a loan from the Bethlehem Lutheran Church in order to cover the expenses that the state was not paying us. Over time, they did pass a budget and made some revisions to the income guidelines that parents were held accountable for. It altered how many people could get approved and it reduced the number of eligible participants in the Illinois Department of Human Services subsidy program.

There was some backlash. People spoke out and said, "This is absurd. You can't expect somebody to make $600 a month working fulltime. It is not even feasible." So, the state went back, revised some things and updated guidelines that were more user-friendly. The changes sought to fit the needs of different parents more than what the originally revised budget was. We have been working with the revised guidelines that resulted in taking away some of our clientele. It didn't take away hundred percent of our clientele, which is what we were originally fearful of. Moving forward, the state has been on time with all their payments, and we don't see any monthly shortfalls or delayed payments at this point.

Now, we are experiencing two things, the first being the processing time for the approval of applications. I have some parents that have come in with their completed application, necessary paperwork and pay stubs to be clearly eligible for the program. However, it takes the state many months to approve them. Meanwhile, our CDC is holding spots for these children because their parents have committed paperwork and paid registration fees. We've now gone six months holding a spot we can't fill, and we're just waiting on the state to process this information. When you call in with questions, it so hard to get hold of anyone down there in Springfield. They're not quick about returning your phone calls. You call in and they say you didn't submit this or that form which you did, but there's nothing you can do. Essentially, it's a waiting game even after you resubmit the information.

New State Requirements for Teachers

We are dealing too with another concern. In order to receive subsidies for your center as part of the Illinois Department of Human Services program, they have now instituted new requirements that teachers must complete. Last summer, I received a letter saying that any person on staff that deals directly with the children, which is everybody in the daycare center, is now required to complete these sixteen courses online within a six-month period. Each of them is an hour to two hours long. You have to provide this information to your teachers and in turn they reply that either I already went to school for this or I don't get paid enough to now continue my education and have to do all of these after hours.

The state department received backlash from different centers, so then they revised the guidelines. Now, you have to complete four courses by a certain date and then the rest of them within the next year. Since receiving the original letter I've been sent five more letters stating further changes. I'm fearful of having my staff complete these courses and then tell them later that you don't have to complete them. It's not a bad thing to have the extra training, but I have a degree in early childhood education. Why should somebody like me have to complete it and then the cook be held accountable for the same requirements? Completing the requirements are necessary only if you want to stay active in the subsidy program. If you no longer want to be a part of the subsidy program then you don't have to complete these trainings. I feel that is part of the governments way of saying we want to weed out some of the centers, so that we don't have to have this financial responsibility.

Advocacy

When we were experiencing the fluctuation in the state money that was coming in, our assistant director Amanda Richoz and I attended a rally at the Larkin Center to state our support for standing together. Something needs to be fixed for the service programs to receive money from the state to meet our needs for this important program. We prepared an advocacy letter that many parents signed before we sent it to our state representatives Michael Nolan and Anna Moeller. We said that what we do at CDC is important, and your support can make sure that these programs stay alive and continue to help members in the community. We received a letter from Anna Moeller saying that she was supportive of us and doing everything she can.

Balance the Budget

When we first started working together in 2006, we went to Bethlehem Lutheran Church for a loan to cover our expenses, and it was paid off in two years. Then in 2015, we faced financial hardship with the delay in state funding, and we secured a loan of $30,000. After some state funding came in, we were able to pay 10K of that loan back right away and then an additional 5K thereafter. We still have about 15K that we owe to the church and continue to pay on the interest and principal to the church. This procedure depends on the CDC budget and how each year goes, how many children are enrolled and what expenses need to be paid.

Regarding the business part of this process, the former CDC director had me as her assistant director, and I was a substitute in the classroom. Because of the financial burden, we were facing, we decided to keep the assistant director in a classroom full time and have the director as a substitute teacher. We hired an outside accounting firm from downtown Elgin. Jim Burress set up new accounting procedures, and one of his associates Marvelle Castic comes in twice a month to prepare payroll for employees and assist with creating budgets and planning.

In building the annual budget, we review the previous year and look at the students to be billed accordingly. For the past couple of years, we broke it down by classroom and looked at how many children that we had coming for the fall. I gave Marvelle the figures as to how much we will receive on a weekly basis, and she pulls out all the administrative fees and expenses. Then we see the breakdown of which classroom is making money or losing money or just eking by. But you can have a perfectly planned budget and then lose five children right after it's done and there goes your budget. Building and balancing a budget is a work in progress throughout the entire year. We are trying to be steady as far as enrollment goes and sticking to the expenses and necessities needed for our program.

Competition for a Key Program

I love our kindergarten program, yet far as being profitable, it is just eking by at this point in time. One of our challenges is that District U-46 now offers a full day program. One of our perks before was that we were not only a full-day program but we also offered before and after care. This is the second year that U-46 is offering a full-day kindergarten program and then they also offer a SAFE program for before-and-after care. The full-day kindergarten is free whereas ours is still tuition based. We found that our program is struggling because parents used to find us a valuable asset for them that is no longer because they can choose a free program.

Our two most profitable classrooms are infant–toddler classroom because there aren't many centers in this area right here that provide infant and toddler care. The other one would be our three-year-old preschool program. Parents are looking to get their children's feet wet before going to kindergarten, and they want them to socialize with other children. They're exploring their options, and our three-year classroom is usually one of our most enrolled programs.

Grand Victoria Foundation

We have not cut any programs or reduced any staff at this time Some of our programs are based on grants that we receive for special programs and they are coming in pretty steadily. Our major grantor had been the Grand Victoria Foundation in Elgin. We have applied to them since 2007 shortly after I took over. We discovered that they offered grants and I worked with Pastor Art Puotinen to create a strategic plan to see where we needed to move within the next couple of years. We based it over a three-year period and that was a significant help to our CDC facility and church programs to put us in the right direction. The strategic plan was essential for us to receive a grant from the Grand Victoria Foundation and they have been a major support for CDC for the last eleven years. They give us guidelines and guidance in grant awards and their management.

Previously, we could apply and receive a three-year grant and then take a year off. Now, it is possible to apply for a grant every year and not have to take a year off. In addition, the maximum request amount has also increased from $10,000 up to $25,000 from Grand Victoria Foundation. We just recently received another grant in the amount of $25,000 for 2018-2019.

Our strategic planning process is continuing every year, and, because it is based on the grant, it has been fun to see where we started and where we've come from. Now, we get to think bigger and outside the box to make our center even better. We need to explore what are other centers are doing that we're not doing so we know how to keep full enrollment. We need to provide professional development for teachers.

A New Challenge from the Fire Marshall

As a new initiative we need to respond to the visit by the state fire marshal. He came in July 2016 to review our operations as a center for the last twenty-two years. He said that we are not up to code in the first floor here with the nursery and then as far as the entrance area. I was flabbergasted because every other time a fire marshal passed us with no citations. Now, we are faced with the challenge of bringing our building up to code. For the last year and a half, we have been working with the state fire marshal, the city fire marshal and an architect to figure out what would be the best way to bring the building up to code in the most cost-efficient way and keep the aesthetically pleasing architecture of the church without changing that too much.

What we're looking at right now is in excess of $40,000 to bring the building up to code. We have to make sure that we get this one problem taken care of first before we go on to do major improvements elsewhere. Just when you think you're finally there, something else arises. You address it because our CDC is a good program and we need to keep it alive.

Exert Every Effort to Succeed

Regarding the new requirements of the teachers to take several courses, as an incentive we compromised. If you complete all of these trainings by a certain date you can have the day off to do anything you wish. Anyone that didn't complete this training needed to come in for that period of time. We had computers and stuff set up here. Well, everyone completed their training by that date. In this give-and-take process we required more of the staff. We value their experience and dedication to our center and provided them this added benefit as an incentive.

In terms of pay boosts, we try very hard but we did not do anything this past year. We had a loss last year so we were not able to do any payroll increases this year. The previous year we gave them bonuses around

Christmas time, based on what we felt was booked and what the final numbers for the year were going to be. The year before that we did do a 3 percent increase in pay, and we also increased tuition at that time. Every little bit helps. We let the teachers know that they are appreciated throughout the year. The board will provide a luncheon for the teachers to thank them for their service here. We host a teacher appreciation weekend and offer other surprises.

Finding Funds and Friends

We value our partnerships with our community. Two years ago, CDC board member Toya Randall said that we need to create a list of donors that can support our center on a regular basis. Forget your candy bar sales and butter braid sales and create a Gala event. We can invite the mayor to speak and charge so much a ticket for people to enter the door and have an auction to raise money for your church. This idea then evolved from there.

Partnership with Good Shepherd Lutheran Church

Our current pastor Carol Book used to be a member of Good Shepherd Lutheran Church in Naperville and is good friends with the pastor and members there. They have a huge congregation with thousands wor-shiping on a Sunday. They have funds to do a community outreach program every year as well to help other churches. Pastor Book got me in touch with their daycare representatives and their pastor. They joined us for a church celebration which essentially was going to be part of our Gala. Our children offered a really nice musical performance, and in the end Good Shepherd made a large donation to our Child Development Center. Then they did a community outreach video and hired a pro-fessional to come and take videos of our daycare center and show our passion for the children. At that time, we were experiencing some of the state issues where certain families were not getting state support. They were able to highlight this one particular story and play it at their church, letting their members know exactly where their money is going.

Giving Tuesday

One other major fund raiser that we do now is done through the Grand Victoria Foundation. We started Giving Tuesday three years ago, an event that happens the Tuesday after Thanksgiving. We reach out to all of our donors, and we've grown over the last three years. We receive donations from them and send our donors three annual letters a year to let them know where their money is going. We include pictures of the children. We do some videos as well. We keep contact with them throughout the year so that we're just not asking for money at the end the year. We send out these letters to invite them to more of our events such as our Spring Fling and our Christmas program. We contact our donors not just to get money but to become active within the Child Development Center. This effort has grown. We are retaining our donors and getting new ones through the use of technology.

Lessons in Leadership

I had courage when I first became the CDC director. As a college graduate with no business experience, thinking and wanting to be an elementary school teacher, I needed courage to be thrown into the director position. Looking back now I ask myself, what were you thinking, but then I look forward. You brought the center from something that was on the verge of possibly closing to a very sustainable daycare at this point in time. I've learned that administrators need to have your ears open all the time, be flexible and willing to work with people: the church, other employees, the parents and the children. There's a whole bunch of different people that I experience every day and you have to maintain good relationships with them in order to have their respect and to have the courage to keep on going.

Bethlehem Child Development Center in Elgin, Illinois

Mission

Bethlehem Lutheran Church Child Development Center (BLC CDC) seeks to provide a warm, physically safe atmosphere of love, concern, support, and acceptance of children in a Christian environment.

Vision

CDC Strives to be:

- A value-centered ministry that emphasizes family, mutual respect and Christian beliefs in a center that helps children grow emotionally, socially, spiritually and academically
- A vibrant ministry that is full to capacity and has the support and involvement of the congregation
- A versatile ministry that offers a variety of Christian education, activity, and care programs to diverse children in a flexible schedule by well-qualified staff
- A very safe, clean and bright environment for growth and development of children
- A viable ministry with monthly revenues above expenses, payment of ongoing obligations and loans based on sound accounting procedures

CDC Programs

Infant & Toddlers, Day Care, Preschool, Full Day Kindergarten, Before and After School Care (ages 6–13).

The Child Development Center offers every child a learning environment designed to foster: SOCIAL INTERACTION, CREATIVITY, SELF-ESTEEM, INDEPENDENCE, SELF-DISCIPLINE.

Teacher guided experiences are introduced to children through weekly thematic units. The weekly units incorporate all of the various learning modalities and include the following elements: Group Time, Story Time, Songs and Fingerplays, Art Projects, Fine Motor Skills, Large Motor Skills, and Sensory Experiences.

While we are a Christian based center, and do not teach any specific beliefs, we feel that it is important for children to clarify their own beliefs, treat others with kindness and respect, build on tradition and appreciate the natural world around them.

Child Development Center Income Summary, September 2016 – August 2017

Total Income	$339,258
Tuition/Day Care Fees	$167,280
Illinois Public Aid Reimbursement	$127,082
Illinois Food Program Reimburse	$ 23,688
Donations & Projects	$ 21,123
Other	$ 21,208

CDC Administration, Staff and Board of Directors

The CDC Director is Kelly Aurand. Eight full-time teachers, two teacher's aides, and volunteers work together with the children. Bethlehem Lutheran Church Resident Lead Pastor Carol Book provides administrative oversight. The Board of Directors includes several Bethlehem Lutheran Church members, parent and community representatives.

CHAPTER THREE

LUTHERAN SOCIAL SERVICES OF ILLINOIS
DES PLAINES, ILLINOIS
CHIEF EXECUTIVE OFFICER
MARK STUTRUD

LSSI News Release

On June 23, 20—Mark A. Stutrud was appointed Chief Executive Officer (CEO) of Lutheran Social Services of Illinois (LSSI) by its Board of Directors on June 23 and he began his work on October 1 at LSSI headquarters in Des Plaines, Illinois.

For ten years, Stutrud had served as president and CEO of Lutheran Social Services of Michigan where he led the organization in overall growth and developed a full continuum of home care services. Additionally, during his tenure there, Stutrud successfully completed three capital campaigns and grew foundation assets from $3.5 million to $13.5 million. Previously, he held positions as vice president for Lutheran Social Services of Minnesota and as executive director of Behavioral Health Services at Allina Health System in Minneapolis, MN.

Stutrud holds a Bachelor's degree in child and human development, and a Master of Science degree in child development and family science, both from North Dakota State University.

Stutrud has long ties to Illinois. His father was a Lutheran pastor in the Chicago area, and Stutrud graduated from high school in northwest Indiana. He has professional contacts and friends in the Chicago area. These ties, as well as an opportunity to position LSSI for greater impact, attracted him to the CEO post.

"It's gospel-centered mission, love for the neighbor, and a full continuum of community services were major factors in my decision to serve at Lutheran Social Services of Illinois," Stutrud said when appointed to his new position. "The work that LSSI is engaged in is an integral part of my professional experience. Home care, behavioral services, and child welfare programs have been a part of my leadership for most of my career. My leadership positions have all been about assessing, leading, and positioning organizations to grow with greater impact in the lives of those served."

Leadership Experiences in Human Services

My career is in three parts. I initially worked for the state government in North Dakota by serving at a human service center in Fargo, North Dakota. Then I worked for the state hospital in Jamestown. I left there to take a job in Grand Forks with the United Health System in a hospital-based program to lead a new chemical dependency program and became the coordinator of developing the adolescent segment of their program.

Then I went to Fargo to work for Franciscan Health Care. They were also developing a new adolescent residential treatment program from the ground up. We took an old convent and did the remodeling and construction to create a thirty-bed unit. It was a great experience, and I stayed there for seven years in different roles with their outpatient work and clinics and headed up their entire behavior health and mental health programs.

Lutheran Social Services of Minnesota

Thereafter, I left the Franciscans to work for the Benedictines in Brainerd, Minnesota. In that system, I worked in partnership with Lutheran Social Services of Minnesota. We operated a joint program together, and I had all of the inpatient/outpatient partial hospitalization programs as well as this outpatient joint venture with LSS. I got to know its CEO and worked there for two years and then was asked to come to Life Span Health system in Minneapolis. It was moving into forming Allina Health System. It had ten to thirteen hospitals that were integrating by ownership into a million-member health plan called Medica. We were one of the first non-HMO, integrated health systems with a million-member health plan as well as many other health plans and patients that we were serving. I had responsibility for the entire behavior health across the system and inpatient/outpatient clinics. We had ten acute sites with thirty-two clinics and five separate outpatient programs. In addition, I worked closely with United Health System insurance. They handled all of our claims, and they did all the back-office and information-technology in support of the operations that I ran.

Toward the end of that time with Allina, I was recruited to work for United Health within their health and well-being division. Once there, I connected with my friend and CEO of LSS Minnesota Mark Peterson. He asked me to be a member of the Board of Directors for LSS Minnesota. Mark and I talked about me doing social ministry work. He encouraged me to give up the for-profit work in the healthcare market to come and work for LSS. I began praying about it and talking with my wife Randy about the open position that he had in mind. Mark wanted me to come in as a vice president and either succeed him or go somewhere else as the CEO within our Lutheran social ministry system.

Lutheran Social Services of Michigan

I prayed about it, sat down with my wife Randy, and considered my stock grants, stock options and executive pay. I could become a philanthropist and be very wealthy from the experience of United, or I could go to work in social ministry. Randy said that sometimes God just wants you to give things up for Him. That's what I did and had many wonderful experiences at LSS Minnesota before going on to Michigan for almost eleven years as CEO of Lutheran Social Services of Michigan and now three years in Illinois.

In my career, I have weathered many storms, developed new programs and done major restructuring within very tough circumstances. In Michigan, we faced the recession, bankruptcy of the city of Detroit, reorganization of the big three (automobile industry), and the state economy in shambles. We went through all that. I also knew about Illinois.

Lutheran Social Services of Illinois

Fred Aigner the emeritus CEO of Lutheran Social Services of Illinois is a good friend of mine. We love to fish together, and we were on the banks of the Puremicat River in 2013. Fred asked me to consider Illinois. They were in the midst of a search, and he was helping in that search process. I told Fred that I had no desire to go to Illinois because it was so messed up there and he told me all about it. We fished a little longer and then stopped for lunch along the shore. Fred asked me this time to interview with the search firm? I said, well because you never have asked me for anything, I will go and interview with them. So, I did and went through a call process similar to my steps going to Detroit. After relying on Scripture and prayer, good Christian friends and their advice, I considered my options. The process for Illinois was much more disruptive because it was very nice in Michigan in that point in my career. I could stay there for a while and retire.

It was clear to me that God was calling me to Illinois, and I remember the day because the Scripture reading that day was about Esther. Her Uncle Mordecai told her to appear before her husband the King to intercede for her people. She didn't know if this was the thing to do. Mordecai told her that it may be for such time as this that you do it. It was an emotional time for me because I had just wept in asking why Lord, would you ever want me to go into such a mess? Little did I know it was way worse than I ever expected. I had no idea we would be in a two-year budget impasse. Who could predict such a thing? It was beyond imagination that a state could ever do such a thing.

Getting Started at Lutheran Social Services of Illinois

When I came to LSSI, it was like storm clouds were on the horizon, and storms were rushing in over the prairie. Lightning was striking, the winds were already up, and we are headed into a structural deficit in the state forever. It meant that you cannot cut your way solely to health and you cannot raise taxes solely. You have to do a combination of fee or tax increases and expense cuts. On top of that situation the state went into the budget impasse and didn't act on a tax increase for two years. They lost two years of opportunity to raise taxes and/or cut expenses. Yet they were paying out the same amount of money while revenues were decreasing, the economy was going down, and jobs were leaving the state. The tax base was reducing. The storm intensified into a hurricane that went from a category one to a category five.

Here at LSSI we had so much in our portfolio of services that was not being paid for because it would come right out of tax dollars called general revenue funds. The state could not pay us because they didn't have the money to pay. At one point, we were at a debt level of 14.25 million dollars on a budget of 100 million so it owed us well over 10 percent of revenues.

We ran out of dry powder. I was just looking over the cliff, never seen it that from that perspective before and hope never to do it again. We were not able to declare bankruptcy because what good would it do. We really had no creditors except for some payables people to put off. Bankruptcy is only good if you can work your way through it, and we didn't have enough to work our way through it. *We didn't have any alternatives but to stop burning cash, to restructure quickly and to monetize assets as quickly as we could to stabilize into a sustainable configuration of service.* Those three things had to happen.

Courage

Courage came into this situation I was facing. Courage is faith replacing fear in my mind. To be given the gift of faith Scripture says is to be given this gift of trust and assurance that I am eternally secure, knowing that I am loved by God, the One who first loved me. Depending on this relationship I know that one thing is for sure, God owes me nothing. That's a sobering thought. God who called me to this position owes me nothing. However, God loves me, so why would God call me to lead and be part of this work only to fail? I began to trust that I would be equipped in some way, and God would manage the circumstances and the things that needed to happen sufficiently so that we would be okay as an organization in ministry. That's exactly what happened. Certainly, God has given gifts to many of us in leadership here and I am grateful for that gift. To God be the glory that it is really in many ways a miracle that we were able to still be standing. There are many pieces to this puzzle that I can't explain how they all fell in place. I could take credit I suppose but that would be disingenuous because I cannot, so I have to say it's faith and trust rather than being afraid and reactive.

Meeting with Governor Bruce Rauner

I met personally with Governor Bruce Rauner in August of the 2015 and told him, if this (delay in funding) goes on toward the end of the calendar year we will be doing major restructuring to be able to continue to provide service. Then in December, I met with his chief operating officer at the time and again said in January we will have to do some drastic things. Or is there anything to say or do so we can be paid in any way so we can continue? His answer was no. It was right before Christmas during the night that the CFO, and I had driven down to Springfield on a dark gray cold day and be told no funds were forthcoming. There was nothing we could do but drive back on that dark cold day and head into Christmas knowing that after the first of the year we would make our plans to restructure our organization.

In the New Year, we made many important resolutions, and I prepared them in a series of Talking Points to announce to our constituents and general public. As a News Release and in presentations we stated the following summary:

Cost Reductions, Organizational Restructuring, and Plans for Renewal

On January 22, 2016 Lutheran Social Services of Illinois (LSSI), the largest statewide provider of social services, today announced program closures and staff cuts throughout Illinois due to the state's inability to pass a budget for the past seven months.

"The state's budget deadlock has severely challenged LSSI's ability to provide services to those in need," said Mark A. Stutrud, LSSI President and CEO. "Over the past months, LSSI has relied on a bank line of credit and available resources from our foundation to compensate for the state's inability to pay its bills. Currently, we are owed more than $6 million by the state for services delivered. After seven months, we can no longer provide services for which we aren't being paid."

The seven-month-long-and-counting budget impasse forced the organization to cut back programs and restructure services as LSSI seeks to bolster resources for the 149-year-old faith- based nonprofit's continued viability. In consultation with LSSI's Board of Directors and an independent advisory group, LSSI created a plan to restructure its services and shore up resources for the viability and continuation of the organization. In all, over 30 programs are closing, and more than 750 positions are being eliminated, or 43 percent of LSSI's total employees. As a result of these closures, approximately 4,700 people will no longer be receiving services from LSSI.

"We are eliminating spending that is most linked to non-payment of services and redesigning our administrative support around a newly restructured organization," said Stutrud. "Our plans respond to this year's budget impasse and an anticipated lingering state financial crisis over the next several years. We're doing this at a great cost to LSSI and those affected by our services. It has been an agonizing process, particularly its impact on our clients and their families who depend on us for their care, as well as our employees whose jobs were eliminated. Many of our employees are direct care personnel who have built relationships and strong trust with the people they serve."The programs that saw the largest cuts were those helping seniors, including home care. Programs eliminated were case management for seniors, adult protective services, and LSSI's Adult Day Care Center in Moline. Although LSSI is receiving some payment through Medicaid, the organization has been accruing several hundred thousand dollars a month in unpaid bills for home care services since July 2015, when the state's budget cycle normally would have begun.

LSSI also has not received payment for programs reimbursed through the state's general revenue fund and other state agencies. These include residential rehabilitation for adult drug and alcohol treatment in Chicago and Elgin, community counseling services, and prisoner and family programs at several locations.

LSSI is grateful for the support of ELCA churches statewide, other faith communities, and donors. LSSI is committed to continuing services that include: mental health, alcohol and drug treatment; Head Start; services for at-risk families; residential programs for adults with developmental disabilities, foster care, affordable senior housing; home care, and programs that help children maintain connections to their incarcerated parent.

"These decisions were the result of a thorough and painful process," said Stutrud. "We know this will impact clients, their families, our employees, and communities throughout Illinois. We made these choices with a long-term view of the organization and its mission, and ultimately the ability to continue serving people."

LSSI Program Reductions

Residential Rehabilitation for alcohol and drug treatment

Behavioral Health Housing Opportunities,
Chicago Elgin Residential Rehab,
Elgin Men's Residence North,
Chicago Men's Residence West,
Elgin Social Detox,
Chicago Women's Residence, Chicago

Mental Health Counseling for children, youth, adults and families

Community-based Counseling in Berwyn, Des Plaines, Downers Grove, Elmhurst, Mendota, Prospect Heights, Wheaton, Dixon, and Villa Park

Youth Services

School-Based Counseling Services, Sterling, Youth Emergency Shelter, Nachusa

Re-entry Services for former prisoners and their families

Connections, Chicago
Employment Skills School, East St. Louis
Homeward Bound Supportive Housing,
East St. Louis River Bend Re-entry, Alton

Intouch Home Care Services for seniors

Canton (serving Fulton County), Chicago (serving Chicago South and Southern Cook County), DeKalb (serving DeKalb, Kendall, La Salle Counties), Freeport (serving Stephenson, Jo Daviess Counties), Moline (serving Rock Island, Henry, Mercer Counties), Peoria (serving Peoria, Marshall, Stark, Tazewell, Woodford Counties) and Rockford (serving Winnebago, Boone, Ogle Counties)

Respite Services supporting veterans and their families

Legacy Corps, Rockford and Legacy Corps, Streamwood

Adult Day Care for seniors and adults 18+ with disabilities

Moline

Comprehensive Case Management and Protective Services for seniors

Case Coordination and Adult Protective Services, Sterling

Talking Points

Budget Impasse and Restructuring

- LSSI has been put in the challenging position of responding to the state's inability to pass a budget for the past seven months and the impact on our continued ability to provide services to those in need.
- We can no longer continue providing services for which we aren't being paid by the state.
- LSSI has been using a bank line of credit and available resources from the Cornerstone Foundation to help pay expenses and cover our payroll. Currently, we are owed more than $6 million by the state for services delivered.
- In all, over 30 programs are closing, and more than 750 positions are being eliminated, or 43 percent of our total

employees. As a result of these closures, approximately 4,700 people will no longer be receiving services from LSSI.

- LSSI's budget of $95 million was reduced to $75 million. Of the $20 million cut, $13.5 million was compensation.

- More than 90% of programs we are eliminating are most linked to non-payment of services, along with those that do not have sustainable funding. We had to look at what we know will be a lingering state financial crisis even when a budget is passed.

- The programs that saw the largest cuts were those helping seniors, including all home care services throughout the state, except the Des Plaines location. Other eliminated programs for seniors were case management (Sterling), adult protective services (Sterling), and LSSI's Adult Day Care Center in Moline.

- LSSI also has significant outstanding bills for programs reimbursed through the state's general revenue fund and other state agencies, and cuts were made here, too. These include residential rehabilitation for adult drug and alcohol treatment in Chicago and Elgin, community counseling services, school-based counseling (Dixon), and prisoner and family programs at several locations (Alton, Chicago, East St. Louis, Marion.)

- In order to reflect the reduction in programs, we also eliminated 18 positions at our Central Administrative Offices in Des Plaines.

- State contracts require that LSSI turn over senior client cases to the state for their redirection to service providers.

- It's important to note that LSSI is committed to a continuation of services that include: mental health, alcohol and drug treatment; Head Start; services for at-risk families; residential programs for adults with developmental disabilities, foster care, affordable senior housing; home care, and programs that help children maintain connections to their incarcerated parent.

Year-to-Date numbers of clients affected:

Seniors

Total number of seniors' services in Sterling: 2,713

- 320 Adult Protective Services
- 2,393 Case Management \
- Staff: 13

Total Day) 2,355 number of seniors in home care: 2,129 + 226 (Adult)

- 406 Peoria (staff: 85)
- 258 Canton (staff: 65)
- 188 Moline (home care) 226 Adult Day (staff: 66)
- 419 Rockford (staff: 114)
- 360 DeKalb (staff: 80)
- 241 Freeport (staff: 69)
- 257 Chicago South (staff: 99)
- Staff total: 578

Substance abuse treatment

Total number of individuals through substance abuse treatment: 912

- 270 Halfway Houses
- 112 Res. Rehab (Elgin)
- 30 Recovery Home

- 500 Detox
- Staff: 53

Counseling

Total number of individuals through Community-based Counseling: 276

- 72 School-based
- 40 Dixon Counseling
- 164 Villa Park + satellite offices
- Staff: 10

Re-entry services

Total number of returning citizens: 791

- 328 East St. Louis
- 164 Alton River Bend
- 44 Connections (Chicago)
- 255 Marion

Taking care of clients

It's interesting that for the most part we were able to find providers for everyone that we served wonderfully. We did not just leave someone in the lurch over someone to pick them up. There may be a few instances out there, but generally speaking most everyone in the 99 percent was cared for by someone else. Take for instance the senior adult population in the home. We had about 2400 seniors sharing life in the home, and every one of them was able to go on to another home care organization. The many for-profit providers in homecare businesses have deep, deep pockets. When this budget impasse occurred from a business standpoint, this was an opportunity for them to gain market share in just waiting it out until they were paid by having deep lines of credit or investors. When we were struggling we could no longer do it because we weren't being paid. The for-profit providers could take all 2400 seniors, take all of our staff and take on any equipment and vans that we had. Take over leases and just grow their business and that's what happened in the home care. In that respect the largest portion of clients involved in our cuts was cared for.

Other people in the mental health programs that we had, if they were close to discharge, we would discharge them. If they were in need of a transfer we transferred them into another program. Not everyone went out of business. What a blessing it is that these organizations are here and stepping up to take this action. Even though I know their motivation is not altruistic, it was still good for the person and for our staff.

ADVOCACY for LSSI

In meeting with the governor in August of the 2015 and again with the state chief operating officer in December, I made clear to them the impact of no state budget and no payments to LSSI would have. In response to our plea for some budgetary assistance to continue our programs, and the answer was nothing can be done. With no relief in sight it became necessary to take the drastic, decisive measures that we outlined above. On that cold, dark day in Springfield and return home for Christmas we faced a difficult future, and we were not alone.

The issue was the impasse and the state couldn't pick favorites. We belong to the Leading Edge Illinois for Seniors Association, the Child Welfare Childcare Association, the Illinois Partner on Disability and Homecare Associations. Every one of them were engaging us as leaders to make visits, call and write, as well as having lobbyists. It became just a constant barrage. I don't think anyone dropped the ball and never let up during the entire impasse. We informed our clients and constituents about the budget by regular E alerts, messaging to donors that we knew were engaged in advocacy, board members and our foundation. We have our annual Lutheran day in Springfield and gather people there annually to meet with legislators.

Balancing the Budget

The process we followed was to restructure to the extent that we were not burning cash by taking three steps:

- figure out exactly where our revenue flow is, where our focus should be, and then make hard decisions to get there.
- sweep out as much debt as possible and do that through the monetization of assets; and
- stay focused and have enough of a remnant or presence to continue in the strategic direction we need to go for growth and do all three.

Here is an example of the monetization of an asset; we sold the Luther Center in Rockford, a HUD supported senior living community of 150 units, to a faith-based organization House of David out of St. Louis. That move brought in several million dollars. I had participated in extensive restructuring in Michigan and Minnesota throughout my healthcare experience and knew how to restructure revenues and expenses along with aligning with new strategic direction. It helped prepare me for the monetization of asset stuff.

We had no reserve fund or contingency fund to fall back on, but what we've done is to have zero debt. Last week we were between $200,000 to 300,000 in our line of credit again, and we don't have any long-term debt as part of the strategy is sweep the debt completely so we can use all our cash toward operations.

Crisis in Organization Morale

People have been beat up for a for a long time. Illinois has been in rough shape forever. We have many staff who been here a while and they told me it's depressing and they are a little-down in morale. They have not gotten much in raises. We had one in 2014; we did a lump sum raise this year but not much. That gets to people after a while. Then on top of it is asking people to do more in the responsibilities where fewer people on board were much more efficient, but that means people are working harder.

We are doing our best to strengthen the relationship with supervisor and staff as a key thing. If my supervisor that I engage with is paying attention to me and helps me understand how to do my work better, tells me when things are going well, and is present with me, it makes all the difference. We are trying to develop a strong culture of excellence with the staff members. We do a lot of training. It's not always about the stuff that's sexy and knowing about the future, but more of how to get better at the block and tackling of your job.

Assistance from Consultants

LSSI engaged with Harney Management Partners' (HMP) in 2016 to assist us in the restructuring and turning around our organization in response to the State of Illinois budget impasse.

Working together with them we implemented a number of key activities to turnaround both the operational and financial performance of the organization, all of which were accomplished outside of a bankruptcy proceeding, and while considering the needs of the clients. These included closing certain operations which were being unfunded by the State ($3.5M savings), transitioning 800 employees to new service providers while maintaining continuity of care ($2.0M), eliminating unprofitable programs ($455K), right size headcount and curb excess spending ($2.0M), sold and refinanced certain facilities ($4.4M), and diversified revenue streams to reduce reliance on the State.

Through various restructuring initiatives, completed by May 31, 2016, the organization's operating deficit ($5.5M) and cash loss from operations ($3.6M) for the year ended June 30, 2016, were forecast to be reversed with a projected operating surplus of $1.2M and net cash flow of $4.1M for its fiscal year ended June 30, 2017.

Harney Management Partners assessed this cooperative effort as follows: "LSSI's core operations were saved, its services to the community were made sustainable, and affected staff and clients were smoothly transitioned to other service providers."

Strategies to Fulfill Mission

We are focused in our strategic vision to be present, responding to the gospel of wholeness and healing to the community. We really have a view for our future of the whole person, and we theologically say if nothing in all creation is hidden from God including every aspect and cranny of us, then we should strive to reach every person. We are expanding our view to whole persons and not just treat symptoms anymore, to be about healing and wellbeing. How do we get upstream to help people so they don't have to be in any type of institution, including foster care, that they are in a natural setting of their choice to live independently and believe they are contributing? That's where we are heading in being Christ in a broken world and responding to the Gospel.

My perspective on strategic thinking comes from being a constant reader and on the Internet looking forward for information and insights. I also have a very good relationship with key leadership throughout the country through our Lutheran Services of America network as well as other networks

A very helpful resource person for our LSSI strategic direction of embarking on the patient as a whole person view moving towards healing is Antonio Oftelie, a fellow and professor at Harvard University, as well as an Accenture consultant. He identifies human services as having a value service curve. He talks about moving from a regulative mode which many of us are in. We administer state contracts with all kinds of regulations so we become so regulative we can't view the whole person. We need to be human service organizations moving to a generative mode from integrated to collaborative in a value service curve. This formula has been critical in our strategic view.

As a new initiative, we finally entered into a new agreement with a managed care organization in the state. For the first time, we are being paid to coordinate care for the whole person and to begin to use social determinants as a part of our network in supporting people. Generally, these are individuals with very serious and persistent behavior health and mental health problems. In the past we were always paid for a fifteen-minute session with someone in therapy. Now, we are paid to coordinate their care and connect them to services within the community. We can provide housing in some cases being paid for this through the Medicaid insurance benefit. There is even some allowance for people we need to help monetarily, and we are able to really do a lot more than we have with this upstream whole person view. This new initiative just started on October 1.

Exert Effort to Succeed

To succeed you need to keep your eye in the future. Never lose sight of strategic vision even though you have to deal with some very hard things. Otherwise, if you're not looking forward or you're looking down or behind, you're bound to fail.

Some personal resources I have to maintain my own energy and effort besides fishing is I like to go pheasant hunting with my dog Gordon. In fact, Fred Aigner and I were just emailing back and forth to go half-and-half on a hunt club north of here in Wisconsin that we can travel to easily in a day and hunt with Seth his son.

I begin my mornings in prayer meditation and having some time in the word of God is just critical for me. I do understand the nature of Adam in the sense of who I can become apart from God. I could say that I wouldn't turn into a megalomaniac, self-centered individual quite frankly speaking without that time with God. I have a tendency to get off on some pretty weird stuff and don't want to be that person. I go usually in yearlong studies or nine months, and now I am into Reformation studies and the book of Romans. I relate to what Martin Luther meant by grace.

Finding Funds and Friends

During the state funding delay, we were able to rely on our LSSI Cornerstone Foundation for the resources in the past three years. We haven't asked for major gifts to help us during the budget shortfall but strategically focused on our future with major donors and asked them to help us invest in our future. We found three families in particular that have been so generous to us, investing huge amounts of money in LSSI and its vision and mission. We are turning the corner with our foundation and they're much more minded about how to develop and draw new donors and allowed themselves to be more in the fundraising function as trustees.

Total contributions and public support for LSSI were as follows:

FY15 $4,862,686
FY16 $6,128,367
FY17 $4,627,210
FY18 $4,216,525 (this amount is unaudited, as our audit of FY18 is not yet complete)

In Fiscal Year 2016, we were fortunate to receive a large bequest, which explains the bump in public support dollars that year.

We communicate in many ways with constituents, donors and prospects with letters, newsletters, and other print materials. I attend Synod meetings to communicate our vision to be part of a national effort called *reframing human services*. In connecting with people and about social service and human service we help them to understand how we are engaged with people in a way that helps them construct their life. It's like a building project of sorts and out of it comes this new construction, a new and different life that really builds in a generative way toward a place where hopes and dreams realized. There is a much greater amount of well-being and where people will contribute because they're in a different place. We talk about it that way and is not this the story of being new in Christ? We are to be a new person, the Apostle Paul wrote, a new creation. This is what we want to communicate how we are a new creation in Christ and how we build our lives. This is what it means to be Christ in a broken world. We are beginning to communicate more consistently like that.

Key Elements in Success

During a critical time, three things needed for success are:

- define reality accurately,
- clarify anything that needs to be clarified, be clear, and
- say thank you, thank you, thank you always.

As a CEO, I must always express my gratitude and thanks to people. We have to help people to understand that when we can publicly recognize them, others are seeing this and want to be a part of it. We do all kinds of social media, we do mail and written pieces, and we do gatherings and events,

Lessons in Leadership

Throughout this crisis and the others, I may have waited too long to do something. A host of factors indicate I could have been faster rather than delaying and waiting just to see if a turnaround or something will happen. Like the budget impasse, I'll get this done next month. We could have been in even better shape if I had pulled the trigger sixty days earlier. At ninety days it would have all been in place so people could understand as well as when it did happen. Maybe not, still it would've been a better executive decision.

Plus, another thing is just trust in God and maintain that trust so you don't have to react in fear and inappropriate emotion and in all the other immaturities that can come out of a person.

There is really no need to get into the politics of the state budget delay because both sides contribute, yet it is political as we look to the future in Illinois. Right now, given its history our state responses only to financial disaster, and it deals with its bonds and bond ratings and not being in junk status. It cannot envision being in junk status and resulting in impasse. If we don't address the structural deficit we will be back in even if there's no budget impasse we'll be back into junk bond status.

I think we are a selfish, self-centered state and what hurts us most is the heart in Illinois surrounds the bottom line. It's rather dark right now but collectively very good legislators and officials need to make good decisions in the face of limitless questions. I view this budget impasse as "a vignette in our book of acts" and we need to think strategically and keep trusting God and our future.

This is an extraordinary time for human service organizations. There is a great deal of momentum nationally to bring greater health and permanency throughout the lifespan, serving in a natural setting— the home. We see this advancing in foster care, adoption, behavioral services, and home care to seniors and people with disabilities. This is the work of LSSI: providing services to people that result in greater independence, integration, and well-being, all while living in their communities.

Lutheran Social Services of Illinois

Mission Statement

Responding to the Gospel, Lutheran Social Services of Illinois (LSSI) brings healing, justice, and wholeness to people and communities.

Overview

Serving Illinois since 1867, Lutheran Social Services of Illinois (LSSI) is a nonprofit social service organization of the three Illinois synods of the Evangelical Lutheran Church in America (ELCA). LSSI is the largest statewide social service provider, serving over 65,000 people across Illinois last year. The demographics of clients served by LSSI generally reflect those of Illinois' population, with one important exception—more than 60 percent of clients report an annual household income under $15,000, compared to just 12 percent of all Illinois households. The organization provides critical programs for the state's most vulnerable residents including foster care, mental health services, alcohol and drug treatment, affordable senior housing, residential programs for people with developmental disabilities, and programs that help formerly incarcerated individuals integrate back into society.

LSSI Summary Operating Revenues for
Years Ended in June 30

	2016	2015
Contributions and public support	$ 6,128,000	$ 4,863,000
Operating revenue	$77,583,000	$81,190,000
Gain on investments and asset sales	$ 24,000	$ 277,000
Total Revenue	$83,735,000	$86,330,000

CHAPTER FOUR

MUTUAL GROUND AURORA, ILLINOIS
EXECUTIVE DIRECTOR MICHELLE MEYER

News Release

Michelle Meyer is the Executive Director of Mutual Ground, Inc., a not for profit agency specializing in working with victims of domestic and sexual violence. Before taking over as Executive Director in July of 2010, Michelle held the position of Coordinator of the Domestic Violence Court Advocacy Program.

Michelle began her work at Mutual Ground as an intern in 1999. Ms. Meyer graduated in 2000 with a Bachelor of Science Degree from Eastern Illinois University and in 2009 with a Master of Business Administration Degree from Aurora University. She has completed sixty-four hours of domestic violence and sexual assault training and has obtained her certification as an Illinois Domestic Violence Professional.

Michelle currently serves as an Aurora Kiwanis Club Board member, is a member of the Fox Valley Credit Union Board of Directors, Council Chair for the Illinois Coalition Against Domestic Violence member of the Illinois Coalition Against Sexual Assault, and a member of the Illinois Domestic Violence Advisory Committee.

A Call to Leadership

I went to Eastern Illinois University for my undergrad and majored in Health Studies. The summer before graduating I had to do an internship, so I came back to Aurora where I was born and raised. I knew about Mutual Ground, and my mom thought it would be a good place to do an internship at Mutual Ground because domestic and sexual violence are public health issues. I was able to do my internship here for the summer while living at home with my parents. Then I went back to school for my senior year at Eastern. After graduating, I returned to live with my parents and went back to the waitressing job at Orchard Valley Restaurant that I did during my teen and college years.

The Mutual Ground executive director at the time was Linda Haley, and she came into Orchard Valley while I was working. I waited on her and she said that there was a position for a Legal Advocate and I should apply. I remembered when I did my internship here for the summer and was able to shadow each department. I really enjoyed my time shadowing the Legal Advocacy Department, going into the court houses and helping people with protection orders, and navigating the criminal justice system. I came into apply and was hired in September 2000.

I remained a legal advocate until 2005, when I was promoted to head that department. Thereafter, Linda Haley pushed me to go even further. She was getting ready to retire as executive director and said, "You could do this job and you should get a business certificate." I followed her advice and went to Aurora University to get a business certificate, enjoyed the class so much that I enrolled in their MBA program. While working full-time at Mutual Ground and one night a week at Orchard Valley, I also completed my courses and graduated with my MBA degree.

Promotion to Executive Director

During the search for a new Executive Director at Mutual Ground, I was able to interview before the Board of Directors. The process was intimidating, as I did not have any experience being an executive director, but what I did have was experience working directly with victims of these crimes. Basically, I told the Board that I would give them my best to run this organization and use what I learned in the MBA program paired with my direct service knowledge. They offered me the position, and I went from being part of the staff to becoming the executive director. Going from ten years in a direct service capacity side by side with forty-some employees to then becoming their leader was a huge challenge for me.

I had to prove myself to the employees here, my colleagues, and that was no easy feat. Some people were excited to have me in this position, but others felt they could have done the job better or that every decision I made was not the right decision. You question your own judgment sometimes, but you eventually rise above all that and just do what is right. I looked to my colleagues outside of this organization for mentorship and help in certain circumstances. I also relied on my key team members to help me navigate situations that came up as well. Along the way there were decisions made that people didn't like because the direction I was going wasn't the same direction of the previous executive director. Ultimately, they decided to leave or decisions were made to allow them to leave if they were not going to move in the new direction.

Five Years of Organizational Changes

We went through a lot of changes in those first five years of restructuring, in losing some staff, and in gaining some staff. It was like a roller coaster ride with some really difficult moments and some really exciting moments. I needed the support of the Board of Directors in this process. They were extremely supportive in my decisions even though there was some conflict among members who had been around for a really long time and newer board members. When I came on as Executive Director, the Board President was dealing with a lot of other things in her personal life and her professional life and wasn't exactly able to be there for me in the way I needed. So very quickly, I had a new Board President.

Ultimately, I knew what I wanted and had a vision of where I wanted things to go. I would lay them out for the board, and the board agreed and supported me in that vision when changes had to be made to keep moving in that direction. We did not have a formal strategic three-year plan; we went year-by-year because in the beginning there was a lot of day-to-day stuff and work that needed to be done. As time went on, I could look up and look further into the future about where we needed to go.

Mutual Ground Vision Statement

Briefly stated we have a *vision statement* to create a society free of domestic and sexual violence. This vision is very broad and not something to be done overnight or even in a few years. It's a guiding light for us to continue to focus on as we respond to societal changes that happen in our environment and provide services and to end domestic and sexual violence.

Societal Changes in Seventeen Years

In the seven years as executive director, and across the seventeen years, I've been at Mutual Ground, I have seen a ton of *societal changes*. In my work as legal advocate in Kendall County and southern Kane County, I saw how huge the differences were from county to county. The Kendall County Courthouse was a lot more rural when I first started than it is now. During the housing boom people flocked there. The population just exploded, and it really went from this good old boys' network to a lot more diverse groups needing help out there.

Societal Changes and New Opportunities

The other change in the seventeen years is that social media has played a huge role in allowing for information exchange, greater awareness, and getting young people on board in volunteering and helping. They are really engaged in social causes and social justice and that's been great. Now we have the Me Too movement and the Times Up Movement. People are paying a lot more attention to domestic and sexual violence in politics and Hollywood, bringing it to the forefront of everybody's mind. This change allows us to think of other possible arenas where domestic and sexual abuse is happening and affecting such as in the workplace, with immigrants and within the LGBT community. It broadens the discussion and opens our eyes to see what was always happening in those communities and groups. More people are feeling empowered, and it's become less of a hidden secret behind closed doors and more people are feeling empowered to bring it in the light. As a result, we are seeing more people are coming to Mutual Ground for help.

Re-Branding Our Services

When I became executive director, our branding was based on our logo. It was a picture of our shelter here which is a big mansion and the tagline was shelter from the storm. As I talked to different groups churches, civic clubs, you name it, I would ask what do you think Mutual Ground is? Everybody would always say, "A battered women's shelter or a safe haven for women." So, we realized very quickly that we need to do something about that, because we provide way more services than just shelter. In fact, out of the approximately 1400 clients we serve a year only about 200 of them actually stay in our shelter every year. This reality brought about the rebranding process.

In the rebranding process we changed our logo, and we got rid of the building. Instead of the shelter in our logo we had just our name with a branch with three leaves. The three leaves of our branch represent *prevention, intervention and ongoing services.* This represents our three-pronged approach to ending the cycles of domestic and sexual violence.

Prevention Education

Our prevention services are in over a hundred schools now doing prevention education programs for kids as little as preschool all the way to seniors in high school. In preschool, we are talking about personal body safety, nobody touches your private area except to keep you clean and healthy. We practice screaming *no* if somebody does touch you in a way that you are not comfortable with. We also identify who is their trusted adult that they would tell if something happened. As we go to various grades in school the approach will be age-appropriate. In junior high school and high school, we talk more about dating violence, sexual assault, and sexual harassment. We talk about social media and the impact of sexting and cyber bullying. We arrange for a private room afterwards so if a child sitting in class and listening to us present thinks this is happening to them, they can speak to one of our educators for help. In a two-month period we had sixteen disclosures of abuse. Getting there early enough where we can possibly intervene and get these children on a different future trajectory is so incredibly important.

Then we go further in our intervention where we will go to talk to civic clubs, to churches and to employers. We speak to employers about what to do if one of their employees comes to them with these issues. We will talk wherever people will have us talk because part of our mission is to provide more awareness.

Intervention Services

The *intervention piece* is the fact that we have twenty-eight beds and seven cribs here on site in our shelter and it runs 24/7. We have two crisis lines that we answer 24/7. We have a legal advocacy program which is where I started. We are helping people in the Kendall County Courthouse, the Kane County Judicial Center and the Aurora Branch Court with orders of protection and civil no contact orders. We are helping individuals navigate the criminal justice system when charges are filed. We are there from start to finish through the entire process. Sometimes, we are the liaison with the attorneys. We work closely with the prosecution, but we are mainly there to provide emotional support and give them information about what their rights are under the Illinois Domestic Violence Act. It's just scary getting out there and talking in front of a judge and the attorneys in the room about something so personal. They're embarrassed about it, so we're there to help them with that.

The final piece of the intervention services we provide is that we also respond to area emergency rooms. We go to Delnor Mercy Center, Presence Mercy and Rush Copley both in Aurora and Yorkville. The nurses in the emergency room call us at all hours, and we will send somebody within the hour to go meet with the victim that is presenting whether it is sexual or domestic violence. Those are the worst-case scenarios obviously because they're in the emergency room. We are there for emotional support and to tell them about their rights and sometimes to tell them about shelter and other options available to them within the legal process. More often than that though we're helping them contact their loved ones, just being a hand to hold, and explaining what can happen next. We rely very heavily on volunteers for that particular program. We run that hospital emergency room program with the help of sixty-hour trained volunteers who are on a to-be on-call. That volunteer is not necessarily ever going to see that patient again after this initial contact.

We enter all our information into a statewide database for our state grants and our federal grants. We use client management software on an internal basis. Anytime anybody comes in for services of any type, even if they're met at the hospital, we're making a record of that contact. Now, that person has a file here so we know what kind of information and resources we gave them. If they call back, we can pull that up again and see what we've done for them. We'll continue to keep case notes on file.

Individual and Group Counseling

In addition to individual counseling, we have group counseling that we do during the day and night. We also have youth and family counseling where we have counselors that work directly with children and working with the non-offending parent and the child to strengthen the bond between the two of them. We do the counseling for the children in the school as well if needed. Our sexual violence counselors will provide counseling for non-offending significant others and family members of a victim. For instance, if a child is sexually abused it will likely affect more individuals than just that child. Mom and Dad usually need immediate counseling.

We also provide counseling to older adults. We've had people in here in their 80s if they are able-bodied enough to be here, and we will serve them. Obviously, there are different circumstances involved with older adults, and we work with elder care facilities as well to make sure that they're getting the resources that they need in the community. Domestic and sexual violence does not discriminate. We have older clients that come in as well. We would like to do a better job reaching out to the population especially since it's going to be on the rise with the baby boomers. That population is definitely a group in our future plans.

The Problem of the Illinois State Budget Delay

Mutual Ground did not receive any state payments from July 1, 2016 through June 30 2017. All providers of domestic services throughout the state thought that we were included in this stop-gap budget, so we thought we were to be paid $600,000. Then we realized halfway through the year that there was no money allocated for Mutual Ground. It caused huge problems for us. We now faced cash flow issues that impacted our domestic violence program costs by $40,000 month.

Previously, our payments were almost always a couple months behind date so this was not necessarily something we weren't used to. In 2015, when the first budget crisis was happening, we came up with a budget crisis plan and decided what we were going to do each month when we didn't see a check. Already in August 2015, we were doing some hiring freezes and canceling some awareness activities. We went into September 2015 and stopped our food coupon program that we had with Marie Wilkinson. They ended up doing it anyway without us so it worked out. We did another hiring freeze, and we stopped all registrations for chamber events and professional development. In October 2015, we lowered our 403B plan match from 5 percent to 2. So, we went month-to-month and just decided on the things that we would have to stop in order to keep moving forward. In November 2016, we finally got to the point where we had to cut staff.

The leadership team making these decisions at this time was me and the finance director, the clinical director and the HR director. We needed the HR perspective in how to work any kind of on restructuring. We had no staff bonus for the holidays and no holiday party. At the end of December 2016, we needed more revenue. I actually went to one of our large private funders and said "I know you want this money that you gave us to be used for ABC, but I need to use it for now XYZ. Can I do that because of what was going on?" Luckily, they were amazingly understanding and said, "Absolutely, you need to keep the place going so do what you need to do." We also asked for an increase in our line of credit from $250,000 to $400,000.

Restructuring Our Staff in 2016

Then in November 2016, we had to restructure and really look at the organization as a whole and where we could cut. We cut four positions in one day: our Infonet person who entered all of our information into the Statewide system, two case managers and one sexual assault counselor. We did a cost–benefit analysis to see how much we would save in each circumstance and decided that it was strategically necessary to make the cuts at that time. We went forward and doing that saved us some money, so we never shut our doors and we kept going. But it didn't solve all our problems. We still had waiting lists of clients needing services because we cut staff who provide the services, resulting in lower numbers that are affecting our ability to see clients on a day-to-day basis. We kept our waiting list only at twenty because we did not want a never-ending waiting list of people around there forever. So, when it got to twenty, anybody after that we referred them to other organizations. At that time, there were not a lot of other organizations to receive them. I imagine it hurt our clients quite a bit when we were not able to see them. It was never really a shelter issue as much as it was walk-in counseling services. People needed that walk-in counseling service and we were not able to provide it for a while. Right now, we still have a waiting list because our numbers are going up. We're still in a rebuilding mode.

Resources for Leadership

To go through this difficult process, I needed resources and help. I went to colleagues in the human services field and other organizations in this area like Ryan Dowd of Hesed House, Eric Ward from Family Counseling, Lynn O'Shea from AID and other executive directors right here in Kane County. They were dealing with some of the same issues that I was dealing with. Even if it was just to vent, to feel validated, to exchange ideas about what each other was doing to deal with the budget deficit and how they were handling it.

I'm not particularly religious, so it wasn't really a prayer thing for me, but I am spiritual in the sense that I have suffered a loss recently that changed my whole perspective on life in general. When that loss happened, it allowed me to take a step back and say okay the skies not falling. The worst-case scenario is the worst-case scenario; you can get through this. So that helped me.

Probably the biggest thing was having a strong finance director. She is meticulous and organized; she kept her finger on the pulse of our cash flow and our budget. I was constantly in contact with her and just discussing ideas. How we can do things and what would be the best way to make a change that will help the organization and have the least immediate impact on the clients we serve and our employees. I'm human and it's not easy to let people go.

The day when we let those four people go was one of the hardest days of my career. We had to roll it out and be very strategic. I went with a proposal to the board on the problem, the money and budgetary issues. I included the savings and risks to the restructure proposal. Having the board support along with the finance director, HR director, essentially my executive team really helped prop me up. It was never like I'm doing this. There was never any arguing; it was very much open discussion with the executive team. If any of them didn't think that this was the right decision, I invited them to tell me why. I needed to listen to them, especially our finance director. She had been the finance director longer than I had been at the organization much less the executive director, so I take what she says wholeheartedly and listen to her a great deal. I didn't always handle it well. There were a lot of sleepless nights. Trying to get out in nature was my coping strategy, and I did a lot of dog walking. Getting out into nature seems to be the best tool for me.

Advocacy Strategies

It was a challenge for me and my social services colleagues to band forces together to meet with the governor or to make our requests for state financial support together. We all do such different work and have a different amount of money that we depend on from the state. For instance, Hesed House doesn't get as much state funding as we do and we don't get as much as probably AID. We have different causes that we are concentrating on and different line items in the State budget. The biggest front that we posed was when we had panels together for press conferences where we would all be on a panel talking about how the budget deficit affected us individually and our clients. We're interconnected so when clients come to see us, it's hardly ever just one issue they're facing but multiple issues. If we had nowhere to refer them for these other issues they are facing, that's hurting us too.

We had board members, staff, volunteers and other community groups contacting legislators. I met with individually with our legislators here in their home districts. We used social media, talked to our funders and did anything to get the word out that we needed help and that legislators need to be put on notice.

We were surprised by the news that in July 2017, we would be paid up. The state paid Mutual Ground in almost bulk style with two bulk sums of the full amount for 2016–2017. So, we went from being completely cash poor to being flush with cash all at once after the new state budget was passed. This had never happened before.

Regarding a contingency fund to help our funding we sought to build a reserve fund ever since I started in 2011 as the executive director. I am proud to say that now we have a reserve fund of a little over four months operating budget so while it is a huge improvement we definitely are not out of the woods. In the meantime, we are also trying to become less dependent on the state so that when something like this happens in the future, we are prepared and are not threatening to close our doors because we've gotten stronger as a result of this difficulty. We have moved beyond this major crisis in the history of our organization. We have now begun strategic planning for the next three to five years.

New Planning Initiatives

Our plan goes beyond maintenance mode to now preparing for new initiatives. We want to change some of our programming to "expand our services" and help more people. For example, we opened our counseling office in Batavia to reach the northern end of our county and then we opened an office at the Kendall County Courthouse to reach more people going there for protection. We just opened up an office at the Kendall County food pantry for counseling in Yorkville and now in a rebuild mode we're hiring more people. Our facilities are not up to snuff; we don't have the capacity in our main building to continue doing the work we are doing and to expand. So, we are looking at getting out of this building and possibly restructuring our programs. Things make it look a little different as time moves on and we attempt to change and grow to meet the needs of our community.

In the technology field, we are now streamlining processes and making it easier for the staff to work with clients. We are trying to get rid of duplication of entry information, to better utilize the analytics that we have, and to show more outcomes of the work we are doing.

To obtain more program resources we are going everywhere to get more grant funding. A lot of it is on-line and we have a grant funder working part time. She does all the research for new grant funding as well as our maintenance grants that we're lucky enough to get every year. But we have to apply every year and do a ton of reports. We've got some new foundations this last year that helped us out a lot. We hope to keep moving in this direction to help us become less reliant on state funding.

We will begin planning in the fall for a capital fund drive. We were able to do a feasibility study before this budget crisis happened and then we had to table it. In that first phase, we learned that we should be able to raise about 2.5 million with the donors we have. We asked our major donors what they thought and received a lot of great information from them. The capital campaign will help with our facilities. All the grants we write are for our programs and helping us fund salaries for the staff.

We just had a trainer in to do training for how to better help transgender clients. It's always good to get an outside perspective in here. More often our staff go off into trainings where they can get CEU's to learn about different things that they're interested in. The counselors may want to go to something about trauma or the case managers may want to go to something different. In our budget, we allocate for each employee to receive a certain amount of dollars every year to use for professional development.

Exerting Effort to Succeed

When we cut those four positions with board support, I had to really think about how to inform the rest of the staff about what just happened. I just wanted to be as transparent as possible about what was going on so I came up with a bunch of bullet points or questions I'd want to know if I was sitting in their seat. So, I just sat down with them all at a staff meeting and said okay you guys know what just happened and here's why the decision took place. I knew that was a question they were asking what is next? It was tough for everybody. They were worried about their jobs at that time so I just gave them encouraging words, constant validation that their work was just so important. Even if maybe the state government didn't think so, we know because we're here and see what happens here on a day-to-day basis and who is coming through our doors. We are making a difference every single day. I think that was all really important because politicians seem to be making such random decisions, and we're in the trenches every day. I talked about what went on at the state capital and going there. I tried to keep them as informed as possible about any new developments I heard from the coalitions about our money.

Communication is key during the whole process. As the executive director, they needed to sense my passion for our mission. It's hard to go through something like this without passion for the mission and people we are serving. The passion just has been there for me ever since I started working with clients that are going through abuse. I see how it could be any one of us at any point in our lives that could go through it, something that is not their fault. They need Mutual Ground just like a fire department. You don't know if it's going to happen. It could happen to your daughter, your mother or your aunt. When it does, Mutual Ground immediately needs to be there to help put the fire out, to be there in a crisis mode or be there for the long haul with counseling to turn a victim into a survivor.

Finding Friends and Funds

We have a Gala every spring and then we have a Walk for Hope every October. In our Walk for Hope last October we had three to four hundred people come to this event. There are families of victims who have passed as a result of domestic violence, and it is an opportunity to honor the memory of their loved one. It's one of our largest fundraisers and also a huge awareness event. Anybody that comes there and sees all the different family and friends walking in memory of somebody who passes because of domestic violence, that makes it more real to them. Also, a lot of our staff and volunteers come to that event. We usually display survivor art or a visual representation of what we do as well.

Then we have our Gala in April. Not everybody working here can afford it so we have a lower rate for staff if they want to come. We usually try to bring somebody in to talk about what they went through and how Mutual Ground helped them or how an organization like ours has helped them.

I generally send notes and letters to people who contribute funds, and we hired an advancement director last February. She's been here a little over a year and she is amazing. Both of our names go on a gift acknowledgment. She's heading up all of our fundraising. She has been very helpful because I can only do so much. She's definitely reaching out to a way larger community than I was ever able to while trying to run the operations. I also hired an amazing clinical director to join our finance director, advancement director and me. I feel like my team is finally one that I can really rely on to allow us to grow in the direction we need to grow.

Lessons in Leadership

Listening is the most important thing you can do; I have done a lot of listening and that's helped me. Also, not sweating the small stuff; I used to sweat the small stuff all the time. Being very strategic in decision-making and not jumping to decisions right away without listening and taking in every possible aspect of things is important. Then also knowing that sometimes you have to be decisive and make a decision when it's warranted. Sometimes, you don't have time, but then making sure that you are transparent enough to inform people why you made the decision. Follow your heart and mind together.

Courage is doing the right thing or what I feel like is the right thing even though sometimes it's not popular. It's not the easiest road, but you know that it's right. When making mistakes we learn from them and not being afraid to admit that they were a mistake. If I make a decision that's a mistake I'm not going to glaze over it. When I admit to a mistake and then think about how I can do things better next time or what I can learn from it also shows the staff that I'm human. I can make mistakes and they can make mistakes and we're all better off for it.

I'm very fortunate that I have a job that doesn't feel like a job. Sometimes, it's stressful; sometimes, it's overwhelming; and sometimes, it pushes me outside of my comfort zone. All in all, I wake up every morning happy to come to work. I don't think everybody's able to say that, so I'm very grateful.

Mutual Ground

Mutual Ground is a safe place where people come together to break the cycle of domestic violence and sexual violence. We are not just a shelter, we are a solution.

Our Service Area

Located in Aurora, Illinois, Mutual Ground serves the Greater Aurora area, Southern Kane and all of Kendall County.

We answer approximately 2,000 calls for help each and every month with 24-hour hotlines staffed by trained Mutual Ground Crisis Intervention Advocates.

As one of the oldest and largest domestic violence and sexual violence service agencies in the state of Illinois, Mutual Ground is the place where the healing begins.

We provide comprehensive victim services free of charge with support from grants, churches, civic groups, corporate and individual donors.

Our Vision is to create a society free of domestic and sexual violence.

Our Mission is to provide education, awareness, and life-changing services that empower individuals, families, and communities to end the cycle of domestic and sexual violence.

Core Values that guide our work are: Excellence, Integrity, Respect and Empathy

Mutual Ground Clients Served for Years Ended in December 31

	2017	2016
Community Education for Organizations	$2,695	$3,956
Counseling & Supportive Services	$1,209	$ 963
Court Advocacy	$1,034	$ 796
Emergency Room Response	$ 172	$ 158
Emergency Shelter	$ 203	$ 220
Prevention Education for Students	$2,575	$2,212
24-Hour Hotline Support	$5,239	$1,983

Mutual Ground Operating Revenues for Years Ended in December 31

	2017	2016
Government Support	$1,193,078	$ 865,832
Grants/Foundations	$ 653,321	$ 463,535
Contributions	$ 260,191	$ 267,241
United Way	$ 56,970	$ 54,760
Special Events/Fundraising	$ 374,837	$ 189,484
Other Income	$ 163,127	$ 114,637
Totals	$2,701,524	$1,946,489

Our Healing Place

In 1972, a local group of women known as the Women's Development Council was concerned about the prevalence of domestic violence and sexual abuse. Some experienced it in their lives or saw it destroying their friends' lives and damaging the fabric of this community as a whole. The idea for a safe haven for victims was born and Mutual Ground was incorporated in August of 1975. The goal of our new agency was to provide emergency shelter for families in crisis and offer 24-hour services to victims of domestic violence and sexual violence. These services initially included counseling, support and referrals to other agencies.

Our first shelter opened in 1978 on the top floor of a property rented from the First Presbyterian Church in Aurora. Then in 1984, Mutual Ground purchased a two-story house on North Lake Street that could serve fourteen women and children. Sexual violence services were housed in a separate building on Lincoln Avenue. The need for domestic violence services surged in the early 1990s and Mutual Ground had to turn away hundreds of women and children each year due to lack of bed space.

A search began to find a building for everyone who needed a place where the healing could begin. We came upon the Edna Smith Home at the corner of West Park and Oak Avenue in Aurora and immediately saw its many possibilities, including a shelter area that eventually could be doubled. The 26,000 square foot building had ample bedroom space and sat on four acres with plenty of grass and parking.

The oldest wing of the building was built in 1853 and there were several additions made over the years. It was in need of drastic renovation that included updates to furnaces, plumbing and air conditioning. An area that was once a church sanctuary needed to be remodeled into offices and group rooms. There were many challenges but we prevailed, and in 1995, following a successful $2.3 million capital campaign, Mutual Ground was able to purchase and renovate the building. After more than twenty years we finally located all of our services together!

CHAPTER FIVE

CENTRO DE INFORMACION ELGIN, ILLINOIS
EXECUTIVE DIRECTOR JAIME GARCIA

I was born in Mexico City and was brought to the US at the age of nine. I learned firsthand what immigrants go through. I graduated from Northern Illinois University with a bachelor's degree in 1971 and a masters degree in education in 1977 and worked for School District U-46 for thirty-four years before retiring as principal of Sunnydale School in 2004.

I came to Elgin in 1970 and was co-founder of Centro de Informacion in 1972 and served on the board of directors since its foundation including many years as president. I became executive director in 2007 and continue to serve in that role.

My service in various organizations include terms on the Boards of Elgin YMCA, United Way of Elgin, Kane County Teachers' Credit

Union, School District U-46 Educational Foundation. Elgin Symphony Orchestra, and Elgin Noon Rotary Club.

Called to a New Mission

I worked part-time for the United Methodist Church and was sent to Elgin to start a Hispanic mission in 1970. With others that worked in the community we saw a big need where people that did not speak English or spoke very little had no place to go if they had a problem or a concern or something. I teamed up with the young Cuban priest at St. Joseph Catholic Church. We went back to our respective overseeing committees and brought up the subject of starting an organization where people can come to and receive the help that they needed. That's how Centro de Informacion got started in March 1972. I was just a green kid coming out of college and changing careers. I was planning to go to medical school and then changed my mind and decided not to go that route anymore. I went ahead and finished my bachelor's degree at Northern Illinois University. That's when I felt a need to help in the community. There was a lot of awareness back then for working with the Hispanic community as well as the Black community. I went to my pastor and asked what can I do? I don't feel led to be called to the ministry, but there must be something that I can do. So, they sent me here coming out of college.

At the beginning, Centro de Informacion was just a joint venture expressing Christian outreach to the community. Then the Church of the Brethren also heard about Centro and wanted to join with us too. For six years we worked together. Then the time came to get more Hispanic involvement. Most of the board members and leadership were Anglo. To get more Hispanic involvement we needed to turn this organization into a more community-based organization as opposed to being a church organization. As a result, we got more Hispanic leadership coming on to the board and that has been our story ever since—come March it will be forty-six years.

I was on and off the Centro board for all these many years until I retired from my job in 2004 with District U-46. When I came back on the board, the Centro director retired, and I was asked as to be the interim director until we found a permanent one which we did five months later. That director stayed on for about a year and a half, and then she saw the need to move on. They asked me to be interim again which I did, and I just stayed on now as the Executive Director.

Major Responsibilities at Centro

As the head of the agency, I have to make sure that everything is running well and smoothly, that we get funding for the programs, report to our funders and seek new funders. I have a full-time job at Centro and am very fortunate to have a good staff. They have been with me for a while now, especially my assistant director Cheryl Wilkins. She has a full-time job and she's been here about eighteen years. My leadership is like being a conductor that connects with many different organizations and works with staff and volunteers to make everybody sing or play in tune.

What I enjoy the most in my work is that there are a lot of new things. It's never the same job every day. There's always something new, a new situation and new people to meet, new relationships to make and new challenges that arise. It is not a boring job. My major challenge has been the funding cuts from the state of Illinois. Since I've been a director Centro has been cut from the state more than $100,000 a year in yearly funding. There was one program that came back and was taken away again. All the other programs have gone by the wayside and have not come back. The Family Counseling Program provided bilingual counselors. People with problems didn't have anybody to go to. Unfortunately, some of our mental health organizations in town did not have bilingual counselors then, but now they do which is a very good thing.

Another program was the Families at Risk program. This program provided counseling services to children in school from kindergarten through first grade. The teacher would see a child with something going on there, and the elementary schools especially didn't have counselors. They have social workers with one social worker for two to three schools. There's no way that they can provide any type of ongoing counseling. Our Families at Risk program was funded by the state of Illinois through the Department of Child and Family Services. We received the names of children having a difficulty and had the parents bring in their child. We would provide counseling enough on a long-term basis to help them get back and make some changes in their life. Sometimes we saw the parents as well if there was some type of family conflict or something that was bringing about these behaviors. Then we would get everybody in here. It was a very good, much-needed program, but there were cuts made from the state to DCFS, and we were cut from that program.

One of the factors here in the community is the growing number of Hispanic families. The percentage of students in School District U-46 has gone up over 50 percent, so the need is extensive. We are limited by funds and staffing like with any not-for-profit social service organizations. If you don't have the funding there's no program. You can have all the intentions of providing a program even if it's with volunteers but it never holds up. Volunteers come and are very willingly want to help. We basically set up a schedule but if a family member from out of town comes, then they have to take care that family member from out of town. Then a need arises and they have to care for them. You really cannot run a program unless you have salaried workers

Advocacy

The current situation in this Illinois budget delay started in 2015 when Governor Rauner began his term. He couldn't get together with the legislature to produce a budget, and that's when it all really went downhill.

The interaction with the governor and legislature to get a new budget is done by Centro de Informacion through a coalition of efforts. We are part of the ICIRR or Illinois Coalition for Immigrant and Refugee

Rights. ICIRR is a state coalition of agencies that provide certain services to the immigrant community. It is not just Hispanic, but Polish, Irish and other immigrant communities that come together to provide advocacy for the immigrants and for the agencies down in Springfield. It can involve going in and talking to the legislators. Busloads of people go down to Springfield as a show of force to inform them of various needs we all are facing.

One of the things I do here at Centro is keeping in constant contact with our local legislators, like state senators and representatives, letting them know what is happening and what our needs are. I contact them face-to-face and by phone. I don't have any writing papers or position papers. I have found that it's more effective to talk to them personally. They also ask me or other leaders of the view service agencies to sit down and talk to them and let them know what our needs are.

The 2016, annual report from Centro is succinct and informative, an important resource for our community and legislators to note our sources of income. It entails not only state funding for Centro but also the funding from Elgin Township, Hanover Township, and Kane County. At this time, we do not receive financial support from the city of Elgin. Fees for service come mostly from our work with immigration. We have immigration counselors help people with immigration issues, whether it's applying to become a citizen or bringing in their loved one, parents or family members to be a legal permanent resident or anything to do with immigration. We do not get any funding for this service, and we need to charge for those services so we can pay our counselors. Our clients provide the fees from immigration.

For example, if someone wants help to become a citizen, we will do all the processing and the fill out the forms. For that service we charge $250 per person. An immigration attorney can charge them anywhere from $700–1,000 for the same thing. We work very closely with the immigration lawyers here in town and have a very good relationship with them. There's enough business to go around. When someone comes in and there might be a glitch, such as the client has a criminal record or some type of a red flag, we have to send the client to a lawyer that can better counsel them. We don't want to get involved, and we have two immigration attorneys in town that we work with. Shirley Sadjadti has her offices right around the corner here on Chicago Street and Melissa Barbosa is the other attorney. We work very closely with them. We have a lot of partners involved in this event, and we try to work with everybody.

In the Centro budget our revenue also includes Metropolitan Chicago United Way fund raising, as well as several annual events. We had an excellent Centro fundraiser this fall; our annual Gala took in $124,000 and other smaller fundraising events are held.

Budget Adjustments

It's been quite a challenge with the state holding up on their funding, and we had to cut a staff member. Unfortunately, when we don't have funding for a particular program, we have to cut staff. When the legislature passed a budget that included our Welcoming Center Program, the Governor elected not to fund it, so we dropped the program and staff position. Our current budget is set until June 30, and then the legislature needs to pass another budget starting on July 1, so we are going to be at their mercy again.

The two Centro programs approved by the legislature and governor received $120,000 in funding. The New American's Initiative program or NAI encourages and helps people to become US citizens. They are legal permanent residents, already deemed by the federal government that they are fully within their legal rights to be here. They have been here for at least five years and are eligible to apply for citizenship. Many times, people don't bother with applying and say I'm just fine. There's no need for me to become a citizen. The purpose of our NAI program is to work with people and help them see the advantages of becoming a citizen. The Trump administration provided the prod to get all kinds of people coming in and asking to be considered for citizenship, and this process is growing.

The second program funded by the state is the IFRP or Immigrant Family Resource Program. We help people that are either legal permanent residents or citizens. If they are in a bind we can help them to apply for public benefits, children health insurance or Food Stamps. With DACA, knownas Deferred Action for Childhood Arrival, we have a lot of young people that were brought here as children or as young people under the age of sixteen that didn't have a say-so in being brought here. A total of 206 young people applied through Centro de Informacion in fiscal year 2016. Since the year 2000, around 1000 young people have applied.

Passion for My Work

I myself am an immigrant. Yes, I was born in Mexico and was brought here at the age of nine. I know what it means to come to another country. I saw the heartache that my parents went through in trying to make a living for us all. When the time came, I said I want to help.

What gives me pride and excitement about the work of Centro are the contacts with the community and the feedback that we get. Many times, totally unsolicited people come in and say that when they were young and came here from Mexico, Guatemala or wherever, my parents came to Centro. You were a big help to enable our family get established and rooted. Now, I am a professional and willing to help in some way. We have had a few people on our board during the years that were precisely that type of person. Now, they are adults and professional; they want to be contributing members to the community.

Recognition of New Citizens

Every year we invite all people that became citizens during the previous year to the last meeting in June of the Elgin City Council. In a ceremony before the city Council meets, we recognize these new citizens. We've had groups anywhere from twenty to fifty people come up. We give them a certificate and they shake hands with the mayor, the city Council members and local state elected officials. It is a wonderful ceremony and everybody just beams, even those people that had no idea that this was going to happen and were just there for the city Council meeting. When it happens, you can see the big smile on the faces of these people that are proud to be new citizens of this country.

A New Location for Centro de Informacion

Centro had been here in this building fifteen years. When the Elgin Federal Savings Bank bought this building to expand their downtown presence, they asked us to be part of the move. They established their branch and main bank downstairs, and Centro received the upstairs location. Elgin Federal Savings gave us a very generous long-term lease. Then the bank was bought out by another bank that sold it to another bank. These new banks have always kept their lease with us and been very generous with us. We could not afford a place like this if it hadn't been for that arrangement.

Unfortunately, PNC Bank saw the necessity to close this branch because they were not making any money but losing money. Closing down the branch that they no longer afford, they're selling the building, and we don't know who's going to buy it. We cannot afford to wait and see who the new owner may be and if they would lease space to us. If the rent would be the regular going rate, we could not afford to do that transaction.

In the relationships we have established in the community we are very fortunate that Presence St. Joseph Hospital *has a building* that they have not used for a number of years. They have offered it to us at a very reasonable rent. It's on the very northeast part of their campus almost at the corner of Lyle and Lin Lor as a standalone building behind the hospital with a lot of parking space. We plan to be moving in around February 15.

At our Gala last September during the live auction part of the program, we have what is called Fund a Need. This year's need was for moving expenses, and people were very generous. We collected around $13,000 for the moving expenses. We feel fortunate because you can't expect volunteers to come in and do it. I would not want a volunteer to come in and lift one of these desks and hurt their back or something. Then you've got bigger problems. The Fund a Need auction funds will enable us to hire professional movers to come in and move especially the heavy stuff.

The Future of Centro de Informacion

I have learned that you can do a lot of planning and envisioning, but you never know what is actually going to happen. I remember a newspaper reporter doing an article, asking me what do you see the need in years to come? I said that maybe there will be a time when Centro de Informacion will not be needed, where people will just be here with no new immigrants coming in and Centro would not be needed. Boy, was I wrong.

Back in 1972, when we got started there were an estimated 5000 Hispanics in the greater Elgin area. Fast forward to 2010 to the census in the city of Elgin alone that year, there were 46,000 Hispanics and now we're almost half the 50 percent of the population of the city of Elgin. Given that fact, you don't know what's going to happen.

Immigrant Housing Issues

Fifteen years ago, if somebody had used the term *foreclosure* who would have known what it is. Today, we certainly know what foreclosure is, and we have to have a special program in dealing with closures because the Hispanic community was very hard hit by foreclosure. There were many people that were duped into buying homes. In the housing industry, everybody was buying houses and the loans were going out right and left. Someone would come to see you and say do you want a house? You can have a house for less money than what you are paying in rent right now. So, some people signed on to loans with five-year balloons, and after the first five years of very reasonable rates, they faced much higher rates and faced foreclosure and lost their homes. You never know what's going to come.

Moving to the Future

Centro has two core programs that we will always have. One is *information* and *referral*. Anytime you have a constant influx of immigrants coming in that don't speak the local language and don't know the rules and the law, they have problems and need a place to go. The other is an "immigration program". Immigrants will need programs to help them with immigration issues. What we do outside of these core programs will depend on what the need is and also where the funding will be.

Three years ago, Centro was asked if we could participate in a program to deal with housing issues. The big banks that got caught with their hands in the cookie jar had to cough up millions of dollars in fines because of housing problems. The Attorney General of the state of Illinois was the recipient of some of these funds and decided to take these funds and give them to community organizations that deal with housing issues. I got a phone call from a person at the Latino Policy Forum. She said you know we can have the funds that are coming in. I know you don't deal with housing but would you be interested in getting it? Of course, I said. This is the way that we get a new program started. We will always be looking for monies for our core programs right, but if something new comes up certainly we will jump at the chance to bring in a new program that is needed. As a good business leader, you have to establish ties and relationships with people out there so that if monies become available, then they can think of you. They can give you a call and ask if you are interested.

Gratitude

Centro de Informacion has some very gracious donors and patrons that are generous year after year. We will receive from five to ten thousand dollars each year. Eight years ago, we started our Community Day Luncheon on May 5 to express our thanks and appreciation to our friends and donors. It happens around the time of Cinco de Mayo, yet the main purpose for the luncheon is to be a "Friend Raiser." We hold it at the Elgin Country Club in a beautiful setting and its dining area with all the windows looking out at the golf course and into the garden. We go there for a nice lunch and recognize people that have been helpful to Centro in that year. We thank people and tell them about our programs or any new developments in the programs. We distribute our annual report and we give a big "Thank You" to everyone. Out of necessity, we have had to change the approach to raise some funds too. We upped the price on the ticket to get in for the luncheon, as well as we started asking for sponsors to have their logo up in front. These are organizations or businesses that are friends of Centro. It is one way of us showing our appreciation. In the fall Gala, we get funds, in the spring we give back to our friends.

Lessons in Leadership

I have always been a people person and a team player. When I started with my staff here or like I started as principal at Sunnydale Elementary, I said to the staff I am not the person coming in here to tell everybody what to do. You're the professionals, and I expect you to continue to do your job. Think of me as someone that is here just to make sure we are going on the right path and to seek your input whenever a decision has to be made. Sometimes when I will ask for your input, we will take a vote and decide together. There are other times when I will seek your input and tell you ahead of time. I'm going to make the decision but I want your input.

We have staff meetings once a month. It's very important to let my staff know what's going on especially when I have such a dedicated staff. Salaries for not-for-profits are not very good. We do not provide medical insurance and any retirement plans, just a straight salary, so I tell them this is a calling on your part. You're here because it's a calling.

Continuing Education

Depending on their position we are able to provide some additional training for the staff. Our immigration counselors receive training at Depaul University law school. The coalition also provides training both for the immigration counselors and for my outreach workers. The staff identifies other training opportunities to attend. We expect every staff person to go to at least three types of training or workshops during the course of the year. For me personally, there's always something going on whether through the city of Elgin, or the new Elgin Human Services Resource Council. The Latino Policy Forum has this wonderful Leadership Academy. It's like the current Elgin Leadership Academy where you meet once a month on the weekends. I attended my first meeting, and it was really good.

Centro de Informacion

Mission Statement

Empowering Hispanics with the ability to effectively integrate into our greater community through the facilitation of information, education, citizenship and well-being

Overview

Centro de Informacion was founded in 1972 in Elgin to help address the needs of a growing Spanish-speaking community. According to the 2010 census, the Hispanic population of this area has risen to 43 percent in Elgin, 38 percent in Hanover Park, and 50 percent in Carpentersville and now, six years later, it is even larger. Immigrant families, regardless of education and income, come with little facility with English and little knowledge of American culture, expectations, and laws.

For forty-four years, Centro has been a place for people to whom language and culture present barriers to build the skills necessary to participate fully in our community. A not-for-profit social service agency, it carries out its mission through: bilingual information, advocacy, referral, emergency food, life skills seminars, legal clinics, parenting skills training, immigration and naturalization services, and programs for at-risk families.

Centro collaborates with the private and public sectors to maximize resources to provide its bilingual, bicultural outreach services. Centro de Informacion is a community-based organization. It is affiliated with the United Way North- Northwest, the Illinois Coalition of Immigrant and Refugee Rights, Chicago Community Trust, the Latino Policy Forum and several other state and local organizations. Centro is recognized by the Board of Immigration Appeals (BIA) of the U. S. Department of Homeland Security Bureau of Citizenship and Immigration Services. Centro is the only BIA recognized agency in the upper Fox Valley region.

Twenty-three years ago, as the Hispanic population of this area grew and the demand for Centro's bilingual, bicultural services increased correspondingly, Centro opened a satellite office in Hanover Park. Fourteen years ago, Centro also began offering services in Carpentersville. The agency served almost 12,000 clients last year among the three locations.

Centro De Informacion Total Clients Served for Years Ended in June 30

	2017	2016
Total Clients Served	13,149	11,854

Centro De Informacion Operating Revenues for Years Ended in June 30

	2017	2016
Government Grants and Contracts	$218,696	$125,444
Fees for Service	$188,423	$181,668
Contributions/Donations	$ 21,690	$ 20,084
Other Grants	$100,744	$137,074
Metropolitan Chicago United Way	$ 0	$ 20,000
North-Northwest United Way	$ 20,000	$ 0
Fundraising Revenue	$114,636	$118,503
Other Income	$ 496	$ 398
Totals	$664,685	$603,171

CHAPTER SIX

ELGIN COMMUNITY COLLEGE
ELGIN, ILLINOIS
PRESIDENT DAVID SAM, PHD

News Release

Dr. David Sam began his tenure on February 12, 2007 as the eighth president of Elgin Community College.

Dr. Sam has outstanding professional career experience. His previous appointment was as president of North Harris College in Houston, Texas, where he was responsible for one of the five colleges and two satellite centers in the Lone Star College System, formerly known as North Harris Montgomery Community College District. Prior to his presidency in Houston, he was dean of the community and technical college as well as a professor of social science and business management at the University of Akron, Ohio. He previously served as vice president for faculty and instruction at Harrisburg Area Community College in Pennsylvania, as well as both acting vice president for academic affairs and dean of natural and social sciences at Mott Community College in Michigan. Additionally, Dr. Sam has held professional and teaching positions at College of DuPage and Harold Washington College, both in Illinois.

A native of Ghana, West Africa, Dr. Sam has impressive academic credentials. He is a cum laude graduate of Illinois State University with bachelor of arts degrees in economics, political science and history. He holds an MA in law and diplomacy and a PhD in international economic and political relations from the Fletcher School of Law and Diplomacy at Tufts University. Additionally, he holds an MBA in finance and marketing from the Kellogg School of Management at Northwestern University and a JD degree from the University of Akron Law School, and an LLM Energy Law and Policy, Center for Energy, Petroleum and Mineral Law and Policy at University of Dundee, United Kingdom.

Dr. Sam is well versed in the complexities of funding educational facilities while maintaining quality in the classroom. Students are a top priority. He believes in the transformational power of education to enhance and change lives and says, "The world is so interdependent that we have to ensure that education is relevant and that students are ready for this kind of world. To that end, I enjoy working with all constituencies to advance the mission of the college."

Dr. Sam is currently a member of the board of directors of the Elgin Area Chamber of Commerce, the Greater Elgin Area YMCA and United Way of Elgin, as well as a member of Rotary Club of Elgin. He is also a member of the District of Columbia Bar, American Bar Association. Dr. Sam and his wife, Julie, have two children.

Getting Started at Elgin Community College

I started here February 12, 2007 and will always remember the day because that is the birthdate of my late mother. I wanted to have her smiling on me. Every year on that day I pause and remember her.

Facing Accreditation Issues

The previous year, 2006 had been very important for the college because we had an accreditation visit from the Higher Learning Commission. They mentioned three things that needed to be addressed immediately by the new president. First, they found us wanting in the way of assessment of student learning outcomes. Second, they said we did a decent job of budgeting and planning, but they were not linked to each other. Third, our current library at that time was a single room, too small for the student body that we had. This matter was very critical because we were cited by the Higher Learning Commission in 1996 to address the library issue. By 2006, when they came back, it was left undone. They were mighty unhappy and gave us three years to address those three issues with a visit scheduled for March 2009.

During the transition to my presidency some work on the assessment matter was done, and in my first year we were able to move that project forward very quickly. We needed additional human resources to work on the strategic plan, so we hired an executive director for institutional effectiveness and planning. This person we hired fortunately was well versed in the Higher Learning Commission accreditation process, and we made greater progress at that time. Library improvements would cost quite a bit of money, and the reason it had not been done by 2006 was lacking financial resources to do so.

Failing to Pass a Referendum

In looking at everything, it was clear that we had to go to the voters for a funding referendum. Unfortunately, in the middle of 2006 we had tried to have a referendum, but it was not for a new capital improvement. The proposal was to increase the resources for the operation of the institution, and it was defeated 2 to 1. The reasons for the turn down were several. The former president was planning to retire, and the money to increase our operations concerned voters who had no idea who was coming to spend that money. The voters rejected it. If the referendum had been for tangible capital projects, people could evaluate the plans. The referendum would have had a better chance of being passed.

I came in with a two-year timetable and still thinking about a referendum to be able to get among many things a library. I assembled a group of internal people with strong support of the board and some community leaders to consider whether it was a good thing to go for a referendum. Our discussions concluded that it was important to go for it.

Making the Case for a New Referendum

My argument for it was that we had buildings that needed to be renovated in addition to the library. The campus was about forty years old, and the economy was beginning to show the signs of a great recession. It was never a good time to ask the voters to increase the taxes. Because the college has the buildings of everything that belong to the community, if there were problems with the community's properties, we have to go to the community and tell them. Though there was a strong school of thought saying you should not go for a referendum, my contention was to tell the landlords or owners of the property what was wrong with the buildings. For example, we had forty-nine roofs on campus that had to be replaced and you have to tell those who own the property that one of your roofs could fall down one of these days. We worked very closely and very hard, and we had very strong community support.

By April 2009, the economy was in a downward spiral and the great recession had started. We told the community that this referendum was going to be our local economic development effort. We decided that the architects and the construction management companies that do the construction were going to be local, and we had labor agreements with the unions for the projects. They all participated in the effort to pass the referendum.

The Higher Learning Commission was scheduled to come in March 2009. Actually, they arrived here on the first day of early voting, and we had the drawings ready of what the new library was going to look like. The vote on the referendum would occur the middle of April, and we were able to resolve issues related to assessment, planning and budgeting for the accreditation team. Everything was done except for the library referendum vote, but they were satisfied that at least now we had a plan to address the library improvements. At the referendum vote in April 2009, nearly 40,000 voters cast their votes, and the referendum passed eventually by 35 votes in favor. This difference of thirty-five underscores the fact that every vote counts and the measure approved $178 million for Elgin Community College. We ended up getting funding for the library, the health and life sciences building, the all-purpose classroom and a lot of renovations on campus. The roads were improved, and we were able to connect West Spartan Drive with Randall Road.

Having Courage to Make Changes

These issues where right on the table for me to address, and my first two to four years were occupied with these challenges. My previous work prepared me for this major challenge. I was president of a college in Houston, and we had wet doorknob construction and renovation, but probably the best preparation for me were two things. *Diplomacy*. I had to work with our various constituencies in the community. *Finance*. A lot of it changes involved money, and the ability to articulate the financial benefits of doing this in the great recession was very important.

Diplomatic training was key to bringing different groups together to get it done. For example, the joining of Spartan Drive to Randall Road had been on the master plan since 1971. For a variety of reasons, it didn't happen. But things aligned in 2008 to 2009, and we were able to make progress and find resources to get it done.

These changes were so fundamental, and we couldn't do anything else without those things being done. I saw a chemistry lab that was from 1970, and we were around 2009, so I asked to what extent are these students able to get the best out of our resources. We have great professors—we still do. They are going to take care of the classroom. However great they are, they do need a certain level of resources, and they were not getting that support. This was so fundamental that I had to find ways of bringing people together to get them done. Maybe part of the improvements was the newness. I was new and going around to various people, talking to them about issues from their point of view and the challenges that they saw to get these things done. These concerns were not only on the minds of the people at the college, but also in the community.

Meeting Major Community Leaders

On my first day at the college, I went to our Fountain Square campus and ran into Jack Shales. He welcomed me and said, "I'll be seeing you soon." Two weeks later Jack Schales and Leo Nelson invited me to lunch at the Elgin Country Club. After the meal, I knew it wasn't a free lunch. They said, "We brought you here because we have an important project that we would like you to consider and do. If you want to be remembered here in this community for doing something good, and if you want to develop a reputation here, the one project that we believe you have to do and is joining Spartan Drive to Randall Road." I said okay. This is an important project for the community to join McLean Blvd. to Randall Road. We in the college had always considered this project being important by the community, so it was easy then to rally support around it. This week on Monday we decided to close early and, in the daylight view you see the normal egress for people to go to McLean and to Randall. A few years ago, it wasn't an option; today people come from that side to the campus, and it's been wonderful. My courage was ensuring that the fundamentals were taken care of for the students so that they can come here on a daily basis and strive towards their educational goals.

Doing Advocacy at the State Level

My speaking, interacting and mobilizing people to pass the referendum and make campus improvements was advocacy at the local level, and then at the state level we faced budgetary problems where there was no budget.

I think the first step in the effective advocacy is not to wait until you need the individuals before you establish some connection. As an institution we have strong connection with our legislators. When you have an emergency, a problem or an issue, you know all of them and have relationships with them. You can pick up the phone and call them at any time, and this approach is at the heart of our success. We have several legislators over the years that we've cultivated and brought here to see first-hand what our challenges are. Then we went with them to solve these issues.

The next thing is not always going to legislators to complain. We were aware of the state's financial challenges. Whenever we went to Springfield, we quickly acknowledged the resources that we need. At the same time, we spent a lot of time letting them know what we were doing with our limited resources. They understood that given these challenges, additional resources could help us do more. We shared information fully with them, acknowledging them and recognizing them. Yes, the money is not there but this is what it means to us.

In addition, we have had US senators and representatives and State senators and representatives come to campus multiple times. They are here for events, and some come by invitation. We have "meet and greet" with the legislators for an hour or more where we make presentations, they talk about issues and answer questions.

Delaying the State Budget

During the budgetary setback at the state level in the first year, the deficit was about 1.3 million, but the net was much smaller. The college has always presented a balanced budget at the beginning of the fiscal year every time in nearly seventy years. With the financial crisis that we faced we knew that the state was expecting to get at least the same amount that we got the previous year. Then there was no state budget, nothing for a long period of time. We had contracts and resources that were dwindling. When the Illinois Community College Act was passed in 1965, the state was going to provide a third of our resources, a third was going to be from local taxes, and a third was going to be tuition. Over the years, the state's portion kept going down, and around the time I got here it was probably around 15 to 16 percent. Then they started going to single digit, and this past fiscal year it is 2.4 percent. Going into that budgetary year we had collective bargaining agreements that we had to execute and were not able to do many other things that we would have liked to do.

During that time, we got into discussions with the college community and were able immediately to freeze hiring and travel and limit even basic resources. What helped us was that three to four years earlier, we had started with a zero-based budget process. When this budget delay happened, we had just gone on zero-based budgeting that we still do today. But the revenue that we were expecting was missing. Everything had been accounted for, but the revenue was not there. That shortfall caused us a lot of headaches.

Making Budgetary Cuts

We had become very successful at what we do and received recognitions for various things, some at the state level and some of them national. Elgin Community College is built like a house, and making cuts is like the game jinga where you start removing pieces. I said yes, we can cut, we can remove pieces, but I didn't know the last piece that we remove when the whole structure would come down. For us, it's not enough being a college. We have a certain level of excellence and expectation regarding student completion. We said that we were not going to touch the core things that help students succeed. We can keep trimming on the side, things like travel, professional development, hiring, and those things that are not the core things that we do here. Our fear was how long will this whole budget impasse go on. You can keep trimming the sides indefinitely, and then we had to look at a reduction in force. We were able to lay off twenty-four part-time staff. Some of them were performing things at the heart of what we do, but we had to cut.

We had some scholarships and tuition waivers that we gave in the past, and we reevaluated them based on what the law said specifically about a certain tuition waiver. The law said seniors sixty-five years old and over at a certain income level could take classes for free. We had reduced it to sixty years old and were not looking at the income. We went back to what the law said that was consistent with what we have done in the past for close to forty years. There were times in harsh economic conditions that made us go back to that original law, and when things improved we went back. We looked at so many things to see what we can postpone for a year and be able to deal with it. By the end of the second year, we have been so successful that we netted $9.7 million in this effort for savings to balance the budget. We are now in the third year of that challenge.

Doing Some New Strategies

During this time, we went back to some basic educational services and policies, and we had been innovative in deciding new strategies. We developed some new educational programs, new partnerships with other educational institutions, and other campus sites that will help us move forward.

Training Emergency Personnel at the Burlington Campus

As you know, the community college responds to needs of its community. As the workforce needs in the area have changed, we have responded to them. We have the new campus at Burlington where emergency preparedness is at the heart of what we do there: first responders, firefighters, EMTs, and police officers. Here, they get the training they need that was not available in this district. Before the new facilities and training at Burlington were started, many officers in this area would routinely go to Champaign Urbana for that training. For example, the firefighter who goes there has a great facility, but first is the cost of transportation and hotel bed there for a week. Then you have a few officers from one municipality in training, and you need them for an emergency back home. They are gone and not here.

Consider the possibilities now at Burlington, fifteen miles from this campus. The cost of people going to Champaign Urbana or Springfield for overnight stay in a hotel is no longer needed. If you need them in an emergency whatever classes or training they are going through, they can stop and join their colleagues in doing their procedures. With this program, we were responding to long-term needs that never go out of style; training for firefighters, police officers, and EMTs so we knew that this was going to be very important. We responded and it was part of the referendum that passed.

Upgrading the Nursing Program

Nursing education was smaller in our building M that we later renovated for state-of-the-art chemistry labs. Because of these renovations,
our nursing program is in now in the brand-new building A. When
you walk through the hallways, it may feel like a hospital because of the
environment. We looked at the long-term needs of the community for
programs that will serve our community.

Expanding Truck Driving Training

Then take the program that existed before I got here, truck driving. We
expanded truck driving because more students go through it, and the
demand rate has always been great because of our location. We are close
to the center of the country with O' Hare airport not far away. It is so
important to ensure that we have trained people to be in the supply
chain in the country. Recently, we identified forklift operations as a new
area where great need exists and we created a program. We are looking
at apprenticeship for long-term needs. For many years manufacturing
went overseas, but manufacturing is back and people are needed to work
in this area. We do not have the labor force, so we are joining hands with
local manufacturers to train the next generation of people who are going
to work there. Many people are looking to their future retirement, and
the companies we are working with are looking for a new generation of
workers. In these hard economic times, we look for programs that will
respond to the needs of our community, are sustainable, and are in great
demand.

Choosing a Transfer Option

Transfer programs are a very important complement of what we do at the college, and we have a large number of students who transfer to other institutions to get their baccalaureate degrees. The cost of getting a first baccalaureate degree has gone up excessively over the years. So, today, more so than ever before, the need to do the first two years at a community college before transferring is very important. Our students transfer to institutions all over the state, and they also go to Ivy League schools. In the past five to six years our students have gone to Columbia, Brown, Cornell, University of Pennsylvania, Dartmouth, University of Wisconsin, Georgia Technology, University of Michigan, Purdue, and one student at Johns Hopkins University. This past semester a veteran graduated in December and transferred to Massachusetts Institute of Technology.

Transfer programs are a good thing; it helps reduce the cost of getting degrees. More and more students are taking student loans. The current $1.4 trillion in student loans is a big national challenge. To make sure that students can transfer seamlessly and go anywhere, we have articulation agreements with many universities whereby students can leave here and go. We get reports back of our students doing as well or better than native students so it is a very important thing that we do and will continue. We also have some arrangements with a couple of universities that we plan to expand. They offer the baccalaureate degree here. Judson University in town offers such a degree program here. Northern Illinois is going to offer a bachelor's degree in early childhood education here. For nearly twenty years Columbia College of Missouri has been offering bachelors and master's degrees here on campus. We would like to expand these offerings because students come and feel comfortable here, they know the campus. They are able to get associate degrees and offering them other degree programs in the same environment is very helpful for them.

We would like to expand with other institutions like Roosevelt University and National-Louis University. In that kind of arrangement, we seek to not duplicate programs and take away from any of them. Transfer articulation is a very important and growing trend. Building more of these partnerships provide a very good pipeline for graduates to go into the community and meet the workforce needs of our residents.

Working with the ECC Board of Trustees

There's only so much one person, even a president, can do so that's why I always say *we*. Even though people give me accolades, we have an outstanding group of people that work here. Let me start with our Board of Trustees. They are a wonderful group of volunteers that provide overall leadership for our institution and are committed to excellence and transparency in everything that we do. They set the broad parameters and utilize policy governance for the college, and they do not get involved in micromanagement. They guide the direction we should go and then I work with others. There is something unique in our board policies that does not exist elsewhere. They have stated that part of my job is to let them know if they are micromanaging. Usually, many presidents get a little skittish about letting the board know, but it's desirable on my part. They are a great board that is connected to the community and have their ears to the ground.

The board meeting each month includes a workshop on the second Monday of the month to discuss the things that they are going to vote on. We make presentations to the board to keep them informed. Then the board meeting for action generally is the second Tuesday of the month. I meet with the board chair on a certain day to make sure that we have the agenda and everything together. Then, I'm in touch with the board chair, vice chair, and secretary multiple times during the month.

Valuing a Strong Faculty

The second group I will mention is our faculty. We have an outstanding group at our institution, about 140 of them are full-time and over 350 to 400 part-time. They are very qualified and dedicated to students and very rigorous in what they do. They get the students ready for going straight to serve in a hospital to serve or to transfer to MIT, John Hopkins, Urbana-Champaign, and other universities. They set very rigorous standards.

Relying on Administrative and Staff Members

We have a strong administrative group and support staff here, and we work together to make sure that we keep moving our institution forward. We have a simple, easy goal. Our mission is "to improve people's lives through learning." Our goal every day is what are we doing to get the students closer to meeting their educational goals. On a daily basis, we look at what we are doing to make sure that we keep going and going. We are fortunate to have outstanding professionals that work together here. Our goals are known to everyone. Our mission is clear and has been so for many years. We keep working on getting more students to complete so that they can move to the next phase of the educational experiences.

Leading a Dedicated Team

I only want loyalty from all to the institution and to the students, so my leadership philosophy is based on loyalty to the greater good of the institution. I believe in a strong team concept and play multiple roles, many times simultaneously. I am the team manager and provide general leadership for the organization on a daily basis for everyone. I'm also a coach to some people, bringing them along simultaneously to play in the game of education and lifelong learning. Since coming here, I've gone for a degree, my number six, studying at the University of Dundee, Scotland for a degree in energy law and general policy. I don't teach now on a regular basis because of time and everything. Yet I am a guest lecturer in classes and then act as a cheerleader. We have a lot of great people doing things, and I step out of their way. As their cheerleader, I encourage and support them, pushing them along. Simultaneously, I consider myself a scout to see what is happening on campus and in the communities. Common in all these things is the ownership of the citizens and residents of this district who we all know are the owners of the team.

Leadership is the ability to juggle many things. I may be chairing a certain group of people doing things and at the same time, trying to coach someone while being a scout out there. Trying to do everything and juggling all of them always will be impossible to do, if I had my finger in everything. Part of my leadership is to empower people. I tell them that this is your area where you work, and you know that we all are loyal to the college and what our mission is.

Building the New Strategic Plan

Our individual efforts then become part of a master plan to guide the college in its growth. On October 10, 2017 the Elgin Community College Board of Trustees approved the ECC Strategic Plan for 2018 through 2022 as the culmination of a year-long period of review that began in fall 2016 and continued through fall 2017. I wrote the following overview.

During this time, college faculty, administrators, staff, students, trustees, and community partners reflected on current and future opportunities through review of:

- Student success data
- Comparative benchmarks and best practices from other institutions

- National trends in higher education
- Labor and demographic trends
- Financial reports.

A timeline of activities undertaken to create this plan is contained in this booklet. Our processes were informed by employee focus groups, student meetings, web surveys, a survey of area residents, and forums of over 100 educational, business, and community leaders. From these sessions, we generated new language for our vision, philosophy on learning, shared values, and four key goals to guide the college's future work:

- Equity and Learning
- Holistic Programming
- Community Partnerships
- Service Excellence and Collaboration.

Our intention is to remain transparent and accountable. Strategies and success indicators have been pre-defined for each goal and provide a basis for the plan-do-study-act cycle of continuous improvement. Progress will be shared annually in progress reports, financial reports, and other public documents. I am confident this plan provides a solid foundation upon which Elgin Community College will pursue its five-year vision, and I welcome your feedback at any time.

Thank you to everyone who participated in creating this vital plan and reaffirming our mission to improve people's lives through learning.

David Sam, PhD, JD, LLM President

Funding the Budgetary Plans

The money coming in from the state is anticipated to be 5.7 million dollars. The student population and tuition has remained fairly stable. Over the last five years our college foundation has recorded its best performances. The balance sheet of the assets and everything is now over 7.8 million dollars. When I came in, it was about three million or so. The foundation has done very well, and it has policies now in place to address anything that needs attention.

In the federal sector over the last decade, we have received numerous grants for the first time even though we have had TRIO grants for many years. We expanded our efforts and then we received the big one from Title III for the first time. Those two components have helped us in our recent financial struggles.

Helping Students Pass Their Budget

As tuition waiver funds dwindled, we have steered more students to scholarships from the college foundation. We also received accolades for our *financial literacy* program that is responding to the national student loan debt of about 1.4 trillion dollars which is a tremendous amount of money. The default rate is skyrocketing because more people find it challenging to pay for their educational loans. It is very easy to get a student loan. Bill Gates can walk in and request a student loan, and we have to give it to Bill Gates. Then someone who has been out of circulation in the world for twenty years could come in and says, I live in your district and want a student loan for $17,000. We have to give it to the person. Ordinarily, all that is needed is to fill out some forms and check some boxes. It's very easy. Sometimes, it's easier to get it done than to get many of the scholarships we offer.

We have been very innovative in handling that situation. About seven years ago, we came up with this program whereby every student that comes in for a student loan has to sit down with an advisor to understand it face-to-face. We have the student develop a budget for the money. For example, a gentleman came in and said he had read on the US Department of Education website that he is eligible for a $17,000 loan. In developing his budget, the first thing that he realized was that this is really a loan that has to be paid back. Secondly, after all the analysis he realized that all he needed was $875.

This approach involves them in a basic game for life, and we take them to the next stage. Students become exposed to what really happens when you pick a career and start working. We usually put up a dozen tables and the students go to the first person who asks what do you plan to do when you leave school? I want to be so and so they give their information into the computer that generates what the average income will be for that field. Then they will go to the next table where Uncle Sam will have his hand out and take out some money. The next table is about the state of Illinois and its taxation. You go to the next table and that is the rent you spend for housing. Then you go to the desk for your car payment and everything else. Sometimes halfway through the game of life the students see where their money is going, the light bulb goes on, and the students have to evaluate their options for life and work. That is a very good program, and we also include some additional workshops for an effective combination.

Receiving National Recognition for the ECC Financial Literacy Program

The National Association of College and University Business Officers, a national organization representing undergraduate and graduate schools picked this program as their #1 most innovative program in 2015. Also, President Obama set up a task force to collect information about the best financial literacy programs being done by schools. ECC was listed on page fifty-four of that White House report and then Department of the Treasury also has a financial literacy committee that includes us on page 18 of top programs. Part of our financial strategy is to educate the students so when they leave here with a diploma or degree they earned, they are going to improve their lives. When so much student loan bills can drag them down, it becomes very difficult for them to realize what they went to college for.

With the combination of these things we've been able to reduce the student loan portfolio of ECC students that they were carrying around *2009 from about $6.5 million a year to today about $2.5 million.* Fewer students are taking loans because of the financial literacy education we provide them. Steering them to scholarships are making important differences for our students and our community.

Elgin Community College

Mission and Vision

The mission of Elgin Community College is to improve people's lives through learning. We pursue our mission by focusing all our efforts on making Elgin Community College one of the best centers of learning in the United States. In recognition of our role as a comprehensive community college, we will strive to create high-quality learning opportunities that respond to the needs of the residents of our district.

Overview

Elgin Community College serves primarily the citizens and communities located in District 509. It includes five counties (Cook, DeKalb, DuPage, Kane, and McHenry and enrolls students for educational programs at its primary campus in Elgin and several other instructional sites in surrounding communities. (See Community College District No. 59 Map below.). ECC programs of study consist of Associate Degrees, University Transfer, Career/Technical, High School Student options, Work Force Development, Continuing Education, and Agreements with other Colleges and Universities.

Elgin Community College Summary Operating Revenues for Years Ended in June 30

	2017	2016
Local Government	$46,048,410	$44,825,156
Tuition & Fees	$24,301,828	$23,830,418
State Government	$ 5,713,131	$ 1,778,546
Investment Income	$ 536,300	$ 446,144
Other Revenue	$ 532,503	$ 554,083
Transfers In	$ 2,738,000	
Total Revenues	$77,131,772	$74,172,342
ECC Total Student Enrollment	$ 10,929	$ 9,918

ELGIN COMMUNITY COLLEGE
Community College District No. 509

District Map

Serving the counties of:

Cook
DeKalb
DuPage
Kane
McHenry

CPSIA information can be obtained
at www.ICGtesting.com
Printed in the USA
LVHW070229030719
623065LV00025B/701/P

9 781949 712452